AF412819

THE F. STANLEY STORY

F. Stanley, about 1970

THE F. STANLEY STORY

By Mary Jo Walker

(Limited to 700 Copies)

March 1985

P.O. Box 1837 Santa Fé, New Mexico 87504-1837 U.S.A.

Library of Congress Cataloging in Publication Data

Walker, Mary Jo, 1932-
I. Title.
    The F. Stanley story.
    1. Stanley, F. (Francis), 1908-   . 2. Historians—
Southwest, New—Biography. 3. Southwest, New—Biography.
4. Catholic Church—Southwest, New—Clergy—Biography.
    Bibliography: p.

F786.S78W35 1984   979'.03'0924 [B]   84-82483
ISBN 0-89016-082-1

Library of Congress Catalog Card No. 84-82483

ISBN: 0-89016-082-1

MANUFACTURED IN THE
UNITED STATES OF AMERICA

The F. Stanley Story is a co-publication of
The New Mexico Book League—*Albuquerque*
The Lightning Tree—Jene Lyon, Publisher, *Santa Fé*

The Lightning Tree   POB 1837   Santa Fé, NM 87504-1837   USA

Dedicated to the brave souls
who attempt grassroots history.

ACKNOWLEDGMENTS

Special thanks to Peggy Tozer, Cecil Clotfelter and Forrest Walker who read the manuscript and made many helpful suggestions; to S. Mary Loyola Maestas, Archivist of the Archdiocese of Santa Fe, and the Rev. Msgr. Richard F. Vaughn, Chancellor of the Diocese of Amarillo, who answered many questions; and to Jene and Jetta Lyon and Dwight and Carol Myers, two great editorial teams.

CONTENTS

Some historians write because they hope their writing will bring them money or promotion or tenure. Some write to espouse a cause. A few write because they must, because it is the only way they can quench an inner thirst or scratch an itch of curiosity. The last class is the happiest, and F. Stanley is in this group.

The term historian has many shadings. Among academic people, a historian is a certified scholar whose commission of rank is a degree of Doctor of Philosophy in history, and whose income results from full-time teaching or writing history. Some of these go on to glory and excellence in their work; some gain renown as researchers or as teachers, become a historian's historian, but find writing a difficult task. Many bank their inner fire when they don their doctoral robes and are content to plod along as routine teachers, living as comfortably as a toad in a puddle of buttermilk, looking upon their diploma as a union card.

The grassroots historian is another type, curious about people and places around them. Their writings are their only certification. Some become antiquarians, with a dilettante interest in ancient things and more curious about precision in minutiae than in the social significance of their subject. The term antiquarian has a different meaning among historians than among bookmen.

Still another type of historian is the buff, an individual who is an enthusiast or devotee of a specific subject. When it comes to sheer bulk of knowledge about a subject, or even to accuracy on a point of information, I have seen many buffs who outclassed Ph.D's. I personally know only three individuals who have their own microfilm readers at home, and all three are buffs. They travel great distances to look at a gravestone or a courthouse record, which is not to say that professional historians and grassroots historians also do not do this, of course.

We owe much to the grassroots historian and the buff. They are the prospectors who discover new lodes. They are curious about people and places and customs, combining the interests of the folklorist and the historian, and if they are good at what they do, they find their work accepted and even honored.

F. Stanley is one whose curiosity and inner fire has drawn him to the study of people and places and events that had gone unnoticed until he saw them. He advanced knowledge in many directions, lit many candles to dispel darkness.

His works are only beginnings, and he knows this. In a sense, history writes itself merely by occurring, and thus there is the axiom that history is not written but rewritten. Another New Mexico local historian, Fray Angélico Chávez, once spoke to El Corral de Santa Fe Westerners and said that history is not a static, pure thing that can be discovered once, written down, and preserved intact forever. Instead, he said, history is a living, growing body that must be nurtured. . .and which occasionally requires surgery.

F. Stanley has wandered across the Southwest like a Johnny Appleseed of history, planting seedlings in the form of booklets and leaving their later nurturing to others. Later historians will convert these seedlings into trees, by pruning, fertilizing and grafting. The work will require more research, more verification, correction and amplification. But F. Stanley planted the first seed.

The historian who uses only *one* source for his work is a fool, but the historian who refuses to review *any* source is an idiot. Any source may have errors caused by lack of information, or poor proofreading, or hasty writing. But some questionable bit of old-timer's lore may raise the possibility of truth; it is then up to the later historian to prove or disprove the fact. Once, when I was gathering information about the New Mexico ghost town of Cabezón, I read an old-timer's memoir that mentioned a stage line running through the town. Nowhere else did I find any mention of this, and I sought to verify the story. A usually reliable professional historian scoffed at the notion that the town had ever been on a commercial stage line. Then a museum curator found a printed timetable of the Star Stage Line, listing the route and showing Cabezón as a stop. Although many dissertations do not list F. Stanley works as sources, the padre's booklets have nonetheless been studied for similar possible clues. Given the time and resources, F. Stanley himself would have gone farther; he leaves that to others.

His severest critics often have been people who never wrote a recognized book, or whose books themselves are not without the flaws of typesetters and human errors, or whose dyspeptic nature made them discard a sculpture because of a chip.

The body of work produced by F. Stanley will become part of the vast lore about the Southwest. It will remain as long as libraries stand and will be consulted and used by generations as part of the grassroots literature. Future writers will correct its errors, just as their mistakes will be corrected by still later scholars. But someone had to start it, and F. Stanley was the man.

Albuquerque, N.M. JACK D. RITTENHOUSE
March, 1984

He was a man of contrasts and conflicts. . .We
are not sugar-coating any of his deeds nor polishing his mis-deeds. Here is a human being. Take
him for what he is worth.[1]

These lines introducing *Jim Courtright: Two Gun Marshal of Fort Worth* might serve just as well to introduce
F. Stanley, the man who wrote them, for he too has many
complexities and has contended all his life with ironies.
An easterner by birth but a southwesterner at heart,
Father Stanley Francis Louis Crocchiola has had as many
vocations as names. As a young man, he entered the
Catholic priesthood against his father's wishes, and for
nearly half a century served his church with great zeal in
various capacities, attempting to balance the callings of
teacher, pastor, historian and writer. Most of those years
he spent in parishes scattered throughout New Mexico and
the Texas Panhandle; several parishes were German settlements where he had little opportunity to use his fluency
in the Spanish language. With limited money or free time,
he also managed to write and publish one hundred and seventy-seven books and booklets pertaining to his adopted
region under his *nom de plume*, F. Stanley. Incidentally,
the initial in that name does not stand for Father, as many
have assumed, but for Francis, which Louis Crocchiola took,
with the name Stanley, at the time of his ordination as a
Franciscan friar in 1938.

Many of Father Stanley's works form a series dealing
with the histories of land grants, ghost towns, villages and
forts. Others tell the stories of some of the colorful figures
who lived in those places: sheriffs, outlaws, Indian chiefs.
Certain characteristics make it fairly easy to identify his

works at a glance. Although the books range from around two hundred to a thousand pages in length (he devoted three volumes to Santa Fe), his booklets are, on the average, eighteen to twenty-six pages long and measure about 5½" x 8½". Most of F. Stanley's volumes have distinctive covers that he designed himself: blue for those pertaining to Texas, golden-yellow with red lettering for New Mexico. But no matter what their color, size, or subject matter, almost all of them carry some variation of his familiar catch-title, *The (Such and Such) Story.*

Privately printed in limited editions of four or five hundred copies and peddled by their author at modest prices, all of F. Stanley's titles now have reached the status of expensive collector's items. But, ironically, he always had to struggle to finance his research and pay his printers. Most perplexing, perhaps, of all the contrasts or conflicts in Father Stanley's life and careers is the fact that, regardless of the value of his works, either extrinsically or as contributions to southwestern history, they have brought him limited recognition.

In his prefaces Father Stanley often lamented the fact that errors inevitably "find their way" into a work of this nature. In the same spirit, the late bibliographer Jacob Blanck once alluded to a Chinese tradition obliging printers to sprinkle a few deliberate mistakes throughout their texts in order to provide careful readers with that pleasant sense of satisfaction that follows discovery of another's shortcomings.

Unfortunately such impeccable courtesy cannot account for any blunders Father Stanley may have made, nor, on the other hand, can carelessness. As Father Stanley also frequently said, in these or similar words, "Pardon the mistakes but say a kind word for the effort." Or, as Browning put it, "Ah, but a man's reach should exceed his grasp, / Or what's a heaven for?"

Portales, N.M.   Mary Jo Walker
April, 1984

THE F. STANLEY STORY

Chapter One

BACKGROUND

". . .this fortune that you want to make"

F. Stanley's own story might rival any that he has
so far chosen to tell. His family were Italian emigrants
who trace the Crocchiola name back many centuries "to
about the year 911." According to Father Stanley there is
a Crocchiola Avenue in Naples and a Crocchiola Square in
Palermo. His mother, Rose Lovico, was a school teacher in
Palermo before she came to the United States. His father,
Vincent, served as apprentice to Rose's father, who was a
sculptor and bronze artisan. Father Stanley says that Vincent Crocchiola was "one of those fellows who like to get
rich quick." Having heard of the Alaskan gold rush, he
saved his money and "in the year 1888 or. . .around that
time of the discovery," he embarked for America. But before he left Palermo he made a solemn promise to Rose's
mother, who had fallen ill. He swore to her "on her death-
bed" that he would not desert her daughter, "even though,"
as she said, "you go to America to make this fortune that
you want to make."[2]

When Vincent Crocchiola reached New York and
learned that Alaska was still several thousand miles away,
"he said, 'the heck with that,'" gave up his dreams of easy
money, and worked at any jobs he could find while strug-
gling to learn English. From New York, Vincent went to
New Jersey, then to Philadelphia and finally back to New
York City. Sometime during this period he studied with the
famous Irish-American sculptor, Augustus Saint-Gaudens.
One of his first jobs involved making bronze bedsteads in
the elaborately wrought style popular around the turn of
the century. Later he "helped make all the New York City
traffic lights on Fifth Avenue, which were the bronze Mer-
cury with the bow and arrow," as well as the equestrian

statue of General William Tecumseh Sherman in Central
Park across from the Plaza Hotel.

Some of his later commissions came through Tiffany's,
the New York jewelers. For one of his largest jobs, he
helped design and cast the distinctively Art Deco ornamen-
tation throughout Radio City Music Hall, including the
bronze plaques embellishing the building's magnificent aud-
itorium doors.

When he had saved enough money to keep his promise
and send for Rose Lovico, "she didn't want to come over;
she was afraid of the water. But anyway, eventually she
came over when her father died," and in 1902, many years
after they had parted, Rose Lovico and Vincent Crocchiola
were married. The couple had eleven children. Louis, their
sixth or middle child, was born on Halloween, October 31,
1908, at 623 Thompson Street in Greenwich Village, at that
time "the art colony of New York City."[3]

Chapter Two

BEGINNINGS

". . .so you figure you're going to show them"

Louis Crocchiola attended public schools, P.S. 95 (later to become a trade school) and DeWitt Clinton High School. In seventh grade he won a contest for a skit, called "East Side-West Side," about life in Italian and Jewish neighborhoods in New York City. "That was the one selected, and that's what gave me the urge for my second vocation, if you want to put it that way," he later speculated. He followed that early triumph by editing his high school newspaper, writing most of the articles and "even poems" himself, under different names, because he had trouble getting other students to contribute. "They were either playing baseball or football or something. . .I loved football, I guess as much as I loved my name, but because of my size. . .I don't think I would have made the football team."

In 1927, probably during the second half of his junior year, Louis made up his mind that he wanted to teach. But because the field was crowded, with "twenty applications for every position," his pastor advised that he "could combine the priesthood and teaching without going on a waiting list." Vincent Crocchiola "was very much against" the idea, and told Louis that he would be the first Crocchiola to enter the religious life in two hundred years.

> He thought that, married, you can help to continue the family; unmarried, the name will die with you. I said "Well, I have other brothers married. They can do this for you." And they have. They have carried on the name.[4]

Louis Crocchiola finished high school and went on to college "for a short time" at St. John's on the Hudson, a Catholic academy in Garrison, New York, affiliated with the Franciscan Friars of the Atonement. He then entered the seminary at Catholic University in Washington, D.C. During his eight years there he pursued a course of study preparing him to teach, and also earned a Bachelor's degree in English. After graduation, thinking he might go on for a Master's, he continued taking as many advanced classes in literature and journalism as he could crowd into his exhausting seminary schedule.

Sometimes he managed to slip away to Old Soldiers' Home for sleigh riding at midnight, or bantam weight boxing exhibitions with the professionals at Maryland's Beverly Beach. "I always wanted to do a little boxing," he later reminisced. "I suppose—being small—you get these sublimations, and everybody, you think, is picking on you, so you figure you're going to show them."[5]

Whether the young man's superiors found out about the boxing or midnight sleigh rides, they said nothing. But they gave him "an ultimatum" that he would have to devote more time to his theological studies if he expected to remain in seminary. "In fact the Superior said: 'Now, either you are going into theology or into English. If you go into English you don't become a priest and you quit theology; if you want to be a priest you quit your English, so make up your mind.'" As a consequence Louis "dropped out of the postgraduate school" and thereafter concentrated on his seminary studies, but still quietly audited a few courses. "Let's put it this way, since it's been so many years ago," he said with a smile:

> I always managed to slip in another course or two without signing my name. Otherwise the bill would go to the Superior, and he would know that I finagled something, and that would be the end of my seminary career. . .Sometimes I think the things I did that I wasn't supposed to do in seminary would make a book.[6]

Chapter Three

WESTWARD

". . .when you've seen the mountains of Taos"

Louis Crocchiola was ordained in the Order of the Atonement, a branch of the Third Order of St. Francis, on February 10, 1938, at Immaculate Conception Shrine in Washington, D.C. At that time, having "an option of taking another name as Saint Paul did," he "accepted Stanley" and likewise "Francis, which is part of the name," thus becoming Stanley Francis Louis Crocchiola. "That sounds very noble," Father Stanley once observed with a chuckle, adding: "You know, in the earlier ages the more names you had the more noble you were." But like his father and mother, in the beginning he had only one Christian name.[7]

Young Father Stanley's first assignment was to teach at St. John's on the Hudson, his old Alma Mater, but three days after ordination, "doctors found two spots on my right lung. They gave me five years if I didn't go to a drier climate." His Franciscan superiors sent him to the Texas Panhandle and a town called Hereford to recuperate. In his preface to *The Texas Panhandle From Cattlemen to Feed Lots*, F. Stanley tells a droll story of his introduction to high plains country in the springtime. After boarding in New York and "what seemed an interminable ride"

> . . .the train reached Amarillo where there was a short stop-over. All was black. We arrived in the midst of one of the famous (or infamous) black dust storms. My hat blew off, and. . .my efforts to retrieve it amused bystanders and people remaining in the train. My immediate thought was to wait for the East bound train and go back the way I came.[8]

In the fall he did go back to New York to teach at St. John's where, said Father Stanley, "in order to save teach-

ers, or for some reason, they piled these classes on me."
For a semester he taught "twenty-seven classes a week. . .
at the college level," including courses in philosophy, re-
ligion, Shakespeare and church history. Aggravated no
doubt by the heavy teaching load, the trouble in his lungs
persisted and Father Stanley asked to return to Hereford.
The climate of the small southwestern town had suited him
better than any he had known, and besides "the Southwest
was already in my blood," he wrote many years later. But
"Hereford was full" and he stayed there only a few weeks
before Robert E. Lucey, then bishop of the Amarillo diocese, assigned him to Lubbock because of his fluency in the
Spanish language. This assignment did not last long either.
As he later recalled,

> Archbishop Lucey had invited the Paulist Fathers to
> Sweetwater, then. . .found out that he could not give
> them Sweetwater because Rome had given it to another
> group. Now he had these priests coming from Los
> Angeles and didn't know where to place them; they
> were on the road. . .He asked me to leave in order to
> give them *something,* so they wouldn't say that their
> trip was in vain. He had promised them Sweetwater
> but they would settle for Lubbock.[9]

Throughout the spring and summer of 1939, St. John's
continued to urge Father Stanley to "come back and try it
again; they had no English teacher. . .The spots were not
really anything to be alarmed about as far as they were
concerned." So once again the young priest returned to
teaching, carrying another heavy class load for approximately a year before he apparently relapsed. This time his
superiors sent him to assist in St. Francis de Sales Church
in Lumberton, North Carolina, but the climate there did
not agree with him at all. Father Stanley petitioned his
governing board, "the Commission of the Archdiocese of
New York," to find a place for him in the Southwest or re-
lease him. "The Board said, 'We have no place; we give
you permission to seek another bishop.'"
He then wrote to Santa Fe, asking Archbishop Rud-

olph Aloysius Gerken to assign him work among the Spanish-speaking of the archdiocese, "and he said, 'Yes.' " Sometime during this period, or perhaps not long afterward, Father Stanley severed connections with the Franciscans and entered the diocesan priesthood, a move that freed him to seek work directly under a bishop. This, he said, "was not difficult to arrange," because he had not belonged to "a major branch such as the Order of Friar Minors." Instead of "solemn vows," members of the Third Order of St. Francis, to which he had belonged, "take perpetual vows . . .something like the nuns do, and any bishop can dispense you from those without going through Rome."[10]

Archbishop Gerken invited Father Stanley to Santa Fe. He arrived there late in November 1940, and waited "about ten days for the bishop to figure out where to locate me." While he stayed as a guest in the archbishop's home, Father Stanley said that he took the first notes for *Ciudad Santa Fe*, the first volume of which he published some seventeen years later. Gerken assigned him first as assistant pastor of Our Lady of Guadalupe Church in Taos, then, in July of 1941, as administrator at San Miguel Church in Socorro. "So that's how I first got acquainted with New Mexico," he said some years later. "Naturally, when you've seen the mountains of Taos you don't give up so easily."[11]

Chapter Four

A PRIEST IN NEW MEXICO

". . .you can't just split"

During the next dozen years Father Stanley served
as pastor of half a dozen parishes in New Mexico. In addition to two separate stints in Socorro (1941-43 and 1949-
50), his New Mexico assignments took him to Sapello
(1943-44), Villanueva (1944-46), Raton (1946-49) and
Pecos (1950-52). Because he had severed connections with
his order, these assignments came directly through the
archbishop of Santa Fe, R. A. Gerken and his successor,
Edwin V. Byrne.

As administrator at Sapello, Father Stanley said that
he had responsibility for twenty-one missions and therefore had to be on the road at least that many days each
month. These missions included, among others, Golondrinas,
Las Colonias, Arriba, Abajo and Guajolotes. In some of
them he said that he worked with Penitentes, and that in
several places he conducted services in both Spanish and
Latin. Whenever possible he attempted to converse in Spanish with his parishioners. "In fact," he recollected, "for
two or three years I rarely used any English whatsoever."[12]

For several years Father Stanley continued to receive
petitions from St. John's urging him to return to teaching,
as well as overtures from various parochial schools in New
Mexico. This troubled him, especially after his health im-
proved. He had, after all, trained as a teacher, his original
order had been dedicated to teaching, and he began to wonder if he ought not to return to it for a while at least. "Do
one or the other," Archbishop Gerken advised when Father
Stanley approached him, "because you can't just split and
sometimes be a teacher, sometimes a priest. I thought you
were ordained to be a priest."

At times, but not as persistently, another old conflict

among loyalties emerged from the past to trouble him. When his brothers and sisters came out to visit, they always seemed astonished that Father Stanley could have abandoned the leviathan metropolis in which they had grown up. "They loved city life; they would look out and say, 'What do you see, what do you want in this God-forsaken place?' " This occurred more often after Father Stanley moved to west Texas, but wherever he happened to be, he could reply sincerely, "If you live here long enough you'll never be satisfied anywhere else."[13]

It was, at any rate, while he lived in New Mexico that Father Stanley began the remarkably ambitious regional writing that over the years amounted to another vocation. The contest that he won in seventh grade, his years editing the high school newspaper, the background in journalism and English that he acquired at Catholic University, had all helped to whet his appetite for writing. Continuing his efforts to write after ordination, he "did a lot of work but. . .threw it away." Then, and later, his associates often suggested: If you're going to write, why don't you write lives of the saints? Why don't you write things of that nature: theology, philosophy? He did try his hand at some articles along religious lines for a periodical that he recalled was named the *Catholic Crusade*. But when he settled in New Mexico he immediately interested himself in historical and regional themes.[14]

Chapter Five

REGIONALISM

". . .Alaska, New Mexico"

During the period when Father Stanley first visited and then settled in the Southwest, the intellectual movement known as "regionalism" reached its peak. Regionalism had political as well as artistic ramifications, the latter involving an attempt to discover and promote indigenous arts in carefully demarcated sections of the country. The movement declined and nationalism took its place after the United States entered the Second World War, but until then it flourished in the Southwest and did especially well in northern New Mexico. Attracted by that area's awesome beauty, rich tri-cultural heritage, and low cost of living, writers, artists and their followers flocked in from all over the world, contributing to an effusion of regional enthusiasm that could hardly help but influence anyone else who lived there.[15]

In Taos Father Stanley struck up an acquaintance with Spud Johnson, Mabel Dodge Luhan and other crusaders of the regional movement. These intense personalities seem to have impressed the young priest from the east, for he praised them in several of his forewords, adding in one preface: "Either I am a fool or I really want to preserve the history of the Southwest for untold generations of Southwesterners yet unborn."[16]

From the standpoint of hindsight, Father Stanley credits the beginning of his interest in southwestern history to several experiences. One of these involved a series of weekly articles that he contributed to the Santa Fe *Register*, a Catholic paper, as a lead-up to a celebration of the centennial of Jean Baptiste Lamy's arrival in New Mexico. The editor gave Father Stanley a fairly free rein to choose his own topics, so long as they pertained to some aspect of regional history. Finding grist for this column, he recalled, "started me wondering—well, why just a weekly article? Why not books?" Another of these experiences occurred while he lived in Pecos, New Mexico, where he often stopped for lunch in "John and Mary's Cafe," a small restaurant run by an ex-policeman and his wife from New York. "He had a little bullet hole up at the top of one of the windows," said Father Stanley,

> and he'd tell the people, "See, somebody took a shot at Jesse James." Well, they weren't going to aim that high, naturally, but I started thinking—Jesse James in Pecos? This I'll have to follow through. . .So that's how I started getting interested in the outlaws of New Mexico.[17]

But his interest in obscure places Father Stanley usually traced to a little paper called the *Pathfinder*. "This paper," he said,

> came out every week. It sold for a nickel, and I'll never forget something I once read in it: "There is no community in the United States that doesn't have a history." Well, everybody writes about Santa Fe, I told myself, everybody writes about Taos. Why not write about places they don't know about: Rogers, Alaska— who ever heard of Alaska, New Mexico—St. Vrain, Bent? You see? So that's how I really got moving on my town series.[18]

This idea became a unifying theme throughout his works. He put it this way in *The Yeso, New Mexico Story* which, as he wrote in 1969,

> . . .may not be important to the man at the wheel try- ing to make it from California to New York in three or four days, but it is very important to the people who call it home or who once called it home. . .Why should it be left only to the student to realize that there are other places besides Clovis, Albuquerque, Roswell, Carlsbad, Las Cruces, Santa Fe, Silver City in New Mexico.[19]

Chapter Six

NEW MEXICO BOOKS

". . .I'd hoped to do five hundred"

Whatever may have sparked his fascination with regional history, Father Stanley pursued that interest fervently. He had some discouraging setbacks. At Sapello his housekeeper burned the notes and preliminary drafts of *The Las Vegas Story (New Mexico)* while he was away for a few days, possibly visiting some of his missions. "She thought she was doing me a favor to clean my desk. All those notes; I had to start over again." Ten years later a similar misfortune occurred when he twice lost the manuscript of *Dave Rudabaugh: Border Ruffian.* "I started over and wrote again," he said, "because I always felt—don't quit, don't quit."

When he grew discouraged and did not know how he could manage to put out another book, he reminded himself of an incident that occurred at one of his missions when he started building a small pizza oven and happened to overhear someone remark: "He'll never finish it; he never finishes anything he starts." "From then on," said Father Stanley, "I never quit." By the late 1960s, twenty years after he started his regional writing, he had "covered pretty well the eastern slope of New Mexico up to Santa Fe, that area. . .[plus some communities] on the western slope. . . and a number of the ghost towns." He had also produced some biographical works and had begun planning a series on Texas. One dealer, Father Stanley recalled with amusement, asked jokingly: "When are you going to die? I'm tired of buying your books." "Well," F. Stanley told him, "I'd hoped to do five hundred before I die."[20]

F. Stanley published his first book about New Mexico, *Raton Chronicle,* in 1948. By the time he transferred to Texas in 1952 he had published four others: *One Mile From*

Heaven Or the Cimarron Story in 1949, *Socorro: The Oasis* in 1950, *The Las Vegas Story (New Mexico)* in 1951 and *The Grant That Maxwell Bought* in 1952. He had all of them printed in Denver by World Press. The title pages of the first three stated that F. Stanley compiled them for the Raton Historical Society or otherwise indicated that the Society financed them, but actually he paid all costs. As he recalled,

> . . .open confession is good for the soul! In those days you could not publish a book without the authority of the bishop, and he would not give authority. But it could be done under the name of some other group. They [the Raton Historical Society] just gave me the name. Never did I have any penny of financial assistance.[21]

From the same source, his own pocket, he paid the publication costs of all his other books. "They're all on my own," he said,

> . . .what I can save, what my relatives give me at Christmas and Easter, plus what my parishioners give me for Father's Day: things of that nature all added up. . .See, most of the times when you hear I'm folding up, it isn't so much for health as that financially I can't do it anymore. . .The way I have to battle![22]

His salary at the time *Raton Chronicle* came out in 1948 was thirty-five dollars a month, making the book a "scarey venture." All of his books, in fact, represented gambles. While over the years his stipend rose, at the same time the costs of printing and research accelerated enormously. As to why he ever decided to publish his own writing in the first place, he observed,

> I read that Hawthorne did this and that eventually someone took an interest. I don't know what made me such a dreamer. I'm still waiting for a publisher to come along and say, "I'll take it; I'll give you ten percent," or something like that. I'm still waiting.[23]

Applications for grants were not successful. "I do regret,"

he noted wryly in *Fort Bascom: Comanche-Kiowa Barrier,*
"that several endowments turned me down so that the poor
became poorer. . ." At one time he applied for a Guggenheim
Fellowship, "four years at $10,000. . .to study the archives
pertaining to New Mexico and the Southwest in Salaman-
ca." He did not receive it, possibly in part because his
superiors may not have encouraged the idea.

> Archbishop Byrne thought that perhaps I would offer
> more as a priest to the people of New Mexico than as
> a scholar delving in archives. And, of course, being
> my superior, naturally he was right. . .I should have
> known better if this was what I really wanted, but I
> didn't know that then. So I'm still in it, and still doing
> the other thing. . .[24]

Chapter Seven

A DIOCESAN HISTORIAN

". . .but you do have to write history"

Father Stanley seemed always to have a lingering concern for the effect of climate on his health, and from his early days in New Mexico he made occasional efforts to transfer to Arizona. Instead, in 1952, he transferred to the Texas Panhandle. "Now, what happened was actually—Bishop FitzSimon's dead now; I guess I can tell this story," said Father Stanley. Impressed with what he had read of F. Stanley's work, and "anxious for someone as interested in history as I was to come over," Laurence Julius FitzSimon, who had succeeded R. E. Lucey as bishop of the Amarillo diocese, approached Father Stanley in Pecos, New Mexico. The bishop was a persuasive man, and Father Stanley vividly recalled their conversation. Said FitzSimon,

> If you believe in climate, I don't see where there's too much difference between Texas and New Mexico. . .as far as dryness. Why don't you come out to Amarillo to work for me? And if you like to write, I'll give you a lot to write about—Texas is big.[25]

When he offered the excuse that he did not know very much about Texas history, FitzSimon brought in a stack of "twenty books that he banged on a table," saying: "That's easy. You want to know Texas history? Here, this is a start on it." Within two weeks, said Father Stanley, FitzSimon came back and asked,

> "Have you got them read?" Anyhow he laid it on the line. He said, "If you don't want to sing Mass, you don't have to sing Mass, but write history! If you don't want to hear confessions, you don't have to hear confessions, but you do have to write history! I'll go all the way with you. . .I know the stuff, but you can write, and I give it to you."[26]

When Father Stanley asked to transfer to the Amarillo diocese, Archbishop Byrne released him saying, "Okay, this is what you want. I wouldn't want to make you unhappy, so go." Bishop FitzSimon assigned him to serve as diocesan historian, with no parish work to interfere with his duties. He recalled the approximate time these began from a cassock which he had made for him "because of my small size; they put a date on the cassock when it's made for you, and the date on that was January 29, 1952. It was mailed from Pecos because it got there [to Amarillo] after I left [Pecos]."[27]

In Amarillo Father Stanley had access to the bishop's large personal library as well as the diocesan collection, and he began reading Texas history "starting early in the morning and staying with it seven days a week, even Sunday." One of his major projects during this period involved the compilation of a work that had little to do with Texas history, however. It concerned Montezuma Seminary, which at that time occupied some buildings constructed in New Mexican colonial-style architecture, and an imposing castle-like edifice, all situated on a hill above hot springs about five miles from Las Vegas, New Mexico.

Operated by the Atchison, Topeka & Santa Fe Railway Company as a health resort in the 1880s, Montezuma's original structures burned twice and were rebuilt, causing the company to rename the place "The Phoenix," but the old name persisted. Over the years the company lost so much money on Montezuma that it finally donated the property to the Southern Baptist Convention. The Baptists operated a college at the site in the 1920s, then sold it to the Bishops of the United States, who lent it to the Jesuits of Mexico to use as a seminary in the long period of conflict between church and state in their country. "Anyway," said Father Stanley,

FitzSimon said the bishops would like to have a history of that. He supplied me with information and I wrote it, a big book, about as large as the Maxwell land grant book, or would have been, figuring from the

size and number of the pages. I never saw it again. . .
and I worked and worked on that.[28]

This work (which should not be confused with a booklet
entitled *The Montezuma, New Mexico Story*) was appar-
rently never published. FitzSimon presented the manuscript
to the bishops and they in turn gave it "to the Montezuma
fathers, who took it back to Mexico with them." Father
Stanley did not keep a copy "because I figured I was working for him [FitzSimon]. It wouldn't be fair of me to
quarrel over it."[29]

Father Stanley also undertook another special assignment as diocesan historian for Bishop FitzSimon. The
Texas Knights of Columbus Historical Commission had begun publication of a multi-volume set entitled *Our Catholic
Heritage in Texas*, written by University of Texas profes-
sor Carlos Eduardo Castañeda with the editorial assistance
of Father James P. Gibbons. Father Gibbons was recalled
by his superiors to Notre Dame, "and. . .when they said
they needed another man to help out, Bishop FitzSimon,
always gracious in regard to historical matters," sent F.
Stanley to help collect notes for the seventh volume. He
spent several months in Austin, and remembers that he
had a carrel on the sixth floor of the tower, which in those
days housed the university's miles of library stacks.[30]

In 1953, "when St. John's College repeatedly sent the
push and the push," evidently after all these years still
urging Father Stanley to come back and teach, "I then
asked for a parish," he recalled. "Well," said the bishop
when presented with this request, "you sure had me fooled.
I thought you were going to come over to be my historian;
now you want to be a priest in parish work." "Look,"
Father Stanley told him, "I was a priest in New Mexico,
and I wrote the Maxwell land grant book and all those
other books you say you enjoyed. I can do that in Texas
too." "Well, maybe so," the bishop replied. "I'll send you
to Canadian [Texas] and see what you can do."

Not long afterward, FitzSimon suffered a paralyzing
stroke, and though he lived several more years, Father

Stanley thus lost the support of a friend and his only effectual patron. He did not regret returning to parish work, "because you see," he observed many years later, "what would be happening there? I would have been brain-washed in the sense of what *he* would want." Father Stanley did seem to regret, however, that he was not able to return to New Mexico.

> I kind of wish in a way (this is just wishful thinking) that I hadn't—well, how do you refuse a bishop? So here I am, and of course I stayed here because once one bishop takes you, then the next one will not take you back unless this one agrees to it.[31]

Chapter Eight

PANHANDLE PASTOR

". . .especially priests speaking Spanish"

Father Stanley's Texas parishes included Canadian (August 1952-55), Rotan (1956-59), White Deer (1959-60), Dumas (1960-61), St. Francis (1961-63), Pep (1963-68), and Nazareth (January 1969-June 1982). In July 1982, when the work at Nazareth grew "too much" for him, the diocese appointed him pastor to Stratford, a village in the Panhandle just a few miles south of the Texas-Oklahoma state line, where he served until his retirement on January 20, 1984.[32]

Considering Father Stanley's Italian background and his fluency in the Spanish language, the fact that several of his Texas parishes were German settlements represents one of the ironies that he has had to contend with in his lifetime. Including English, Italian, Spanish, and of course Latin, Father Stanley "at one time. . .had a working knowledge of about eleven languages." He did not speak German, however, though he said that he often wished he could at least read it, "because there are a lot of wonderful works in German regarding the high plains country." Reflecting further on this situation, he added,

> Like the army, isn't it? . . .It's not what you want, but what they tell you to do. Well, that's life for you . . .For some reason or other, to give one of another nationality to a parish seems to work better. And that's all right. There is such a shortage of priests anyway —especially priests speaking Spanish.[33]

Rodeo Town (Canadian Texas), F. Stanley's first book about Texas, came out in 1953. One of his major efforts, it it is a full-dress history of the town and Hemphill County. He also published two other full-length works in 1953, but both of these dealt with New Mexico: *Desperadoes of New Mexico* and *Fort Union (New Mexico)*. He published only one other book pertaining to Texas during the remainder of the next two decades: *Jim Courtright: Two Gun Marshal of Fort Worth*, in 1957. This was preceded in 1956 by his book about regional outlaw *Clay Allison*, a character who also had a prominent place in other F. Stanley books, among them *The Grant That Maxwell Bought* and the above mentioned *Desperadoes*. In 1958 he published the second of his "outlaw" series, *No Tears for Black Jack Ketchum*, and the first of his trilogy, *Ciudad Santa Fe*. In 1959 he brought out *Ike Stockton*, a book pertaining to New Mexico's county wars.

These eight titles comprised his total published output in the eight-year period from 1953 through 1960 (later he often averaged that many or more per year), but all represented major efforts. All were fairly well written, some in almost novelistic style with imaginary dialogue. They also had photographs, bibliographies or appendices; features that take time to assemble and that result in higher publication costs. Father Stanley liked to paint for relaxation, primarily landscapes, but his only book to include one of his paintings featured his portrait of General Sumner. Not until the 1960s, when he launched his "place series," did he begin pounding out six, seven or more publications every year; and not until 1971, despite his assurances to FitzSimon, did he put out another book about Texas.[34]

Over the years Father Stanley's topics seemed to fall into several categories, or mini-series: the place booklets (including those on Texas as well as New Mexico); a group of works on southwestern outlaws and Indians; a few general biographies; and three works evidently beginning a new series surveying broad topics (see page 41). In terms of quick sales, his most successful books were *Clay Allison* and *The Apaches of New Mexico*, published in 1956 and 1962 respectively. Regarding *Clay Allison*, he said that "in one week five hundred copies were gone." As for *The Apaches*, he thought that he probably could have sold five thousand, ten times the number of copies he had printed.

In fact, whether pertaining to single individuals or nations, all but one of his books about Indians sold speedily. The exception was *The Jicarilla Apaches of New Mexico,* issued in 1967. Father Stanley had counted on sales among the Jicarillas to put the publication in the black, but they "took only fifty copies." Also with one exception, *Early Days of the Oil Industry in the Texas Panhandle,* which he offered for less than cost at six dollars a copy, F. Stanley's books and booklets on Texas sold quickly too. As he surmised:

> Whether it's because Texas is such a vast state, or whether it's because it has laws requiring the teaching of Texas history in the schools. . .Texans are history conscious, and perhaps this is why my Texas books go faster in Texas than New Mexico books do there.[35]

The Civil War in New Mexico was one of the slowest sellers among his books, though its appearance in 1960 coincided with the beginning of the centennial anniversary of that conflict, and a subsequent resurgence of national interest in it. He said that he gave most of the copies away and, according to his bookkeeping, lost $1,600 on it. Nine years after its publication he still owed the printer ninety-one dollars.[36]

Chapter Nine

TRANSITIONS

". . .maybe New Mexico was saturated with me"

At times F. Stanley has claimed New Mexico as "my first love, really." At other times, toward the end of his writing career, he maintained that the very name "Texas Panhandle" always fascinated him, that he "wanted to write about Texas, but someone advised that Texas had lots of writers while New Mexico needed more." In his last book so far published, he wrote: "You have to live but a short time in the Panhandle to realize that whatever the drawbacks you are captivated, enslaved, and you know deep in your heart that for you there is no other place to live." And in an interview in 1975 he said: "I felt perhaps —maybe New Mexico was saturated with me, rather than I saturated with this beautiful history."[37]

Considering the circumstances, one would have expected Father Stanley's interest in New Mexico to taper off long before then. Among these circumstances there were his continual financial struggles, bouts with ill health and the increasing infirmities of age, the indifference toward his contributions that he encountered in New Mexico, and distance. As his assignments took him farther north and east into Panhandle country, he could no longer make a research trip to New Mexico in two or three days as he had often done before. But he did not abandon loyalties easily. Out of a total of one hundred and seventy-seven books, only around two dozen concerned Texas. Books about New Mexico continued to emerge from his manual typewriter in an apparently never-ending stream, until November 1973 when he published his last so far on that state: *The San Antonio (New Mexico) Story.*

During the early 1970s, nearly twenty years after *Rodeo Town* came out, Father Stanley began once again to write about Texas. But now a further change in emphasis appeared, brought about by an unforeseen circumstance. This new factor was the approaching United States bicentennial and its effect on community self-consciousness in the Southwest, where regionalism had lately flourished. Towns and cities throughout the region began hopping aboard the local history bandwagon, and F. Stanley found that "Every county in the Panhandle already has or soon will publish a county history through the county historical society."

From 1971 to 1976, interspersed by booklets about Panhandle places such as Lefors, Silverton, Higgins, Phillips, Skellytown, Texline and some fifteen others, he published his three long surveys: *The Texas Panhandle From Cattlemen to Feed Lots, The Early Days of the Oil Industry in the Texas Panhandle* and *The Story of the Texas Panhandle Railroads*. Book jackets and prefaces in the 1970s announced forthcoming works dealing with more surveys along the same line, such as newspapers and education in Texas, and military posts and railroads in New Mexico. F. Stanley, in other words, had not yet entirely abandoned New Mexico in his plans, but he did intend to devote less time to towns or individuals than he had done in the past. Unfortunately, the three titles mentioned above seemed also to signal the end of his writing career. Although he recently wrote from his parish in Stratford, Texas, "I AM HOPING TO GET BACK AT WRITING IF OLD AGE DOESN'T GET ME" [capitalization his], he has published nothing since 1976.[38]

Chapter Ten

KEEPING THE RECORD

". . .even the name will be forgotten"

Aside from the success or failure of individual works, Father Stanley's reputation rests to a large extent on his "place booklets," the paperbound series dealing with often obscure towns, villages or ghost towns that he usually entitled *The (Such and Such) Story* and began publishing around 1960. Of course the first six or seven books by F. Stanley concerned places, or at least territory. His fifth, *The Grant That Maxwell Bought*, had two long chapters in which he sketched the histories of towns built on the grant: Catskill, Brilliant, Elizabethtown, Dawson, Raton, Springer and others. Very likely he developed these sketches from material he had used in his column for the Santa Fe *Register*, and this material probably furnished a start later on for booklets about the same towns in his place series.

At any rate, Father Stanley never bothered to keep a record of his publications and, always more place-than-time oriented, he does not recall their dates or sequence with any certainty. Six of his earliest booklets had no title pages and therefore no publication data. Among these six were *The Alma (New Mexico) Story, The Antonchico (New Mexico) Story, The Abiquiu (New Mexico) Story, The Clayton (New Mexico) Story* and *The White Oaks (New Mexico) Story. The San Marcial (New Mexico) Story*, though it also had no title page, began with a foreword datelined "White Deer, Texas, May 31, 1960." Another, *The Fort Fillmore, New Mexico Story*, had no datelined foreword, but was the first of the booklets to include a title page, and this established the date of publication as May 1960. Both the Fort Fillmore and San Marcial stories were followed in the same year (1960) by four others, complete with title pages and dates, concerning Kingston, Dawson, Shakespeare and Los Alamos. Scores of others came out over the next fifteen years. F. Stanley regarded them as a series, as he indicated in the foreword to the San Marcial story, and he dated them serially with month as well as year of publication.

While the Fort Fillmore booklet (dated May 1960) could have preceded the San Marcial booklet (datelined May 31, 1960), the foreword included in the latter indicates that it was intended as the first of the series. In this foreword, F. Stanley briefly presented his plans and rationale. He stated that he intended to issue a "series" of works concerning small towns in "the Southwest, especially in New Mexico" because of the difficulty in finding much published information about them. Two hundred, he estimated, would pertain to ghost towns. "If some sort of record is not kept," he wrote,

> even the name will be forgotten. . .For this reason we are putting out this series of booklets to enable the antiquarian, collector, research student, librarian with some background about these elusive names [sic]. Such places are too small for a large book and too large for a pamphlet, hence the booklet. . .We hope that this the first in the series meets with your approval.[39]

The foreword went on to list as forthcoming the booklets on Alma, Antonchico and Fort Fillmore mentioned above, plus San Antonito, Costilla, Carthage, "and so many others buried in the forgotten past." The last three remain as yet unpublished. Jack Rittenhouse has noted that F. Stanley "often mentioned works in progress, sometimes with 'scheduled' dates." These titles Rittenhouse called "ghost works," surmising that they "were sidetracked when other writings blossomed or when funds or health ran short." For instance, F. Stanley projected booklets on Nogal, Farmington, Hobbs, Jemez Pueblo, Borger, Pampa, Hereford, and many, many others that he never printed.[40]

Chapter Eleven

PATTERNS AND PLANS

". . .if the good Lord is going to let me"

Regardless of their exact sequence, F. Stanley used the "editorial we" throughout most of his booklets, as indeed he did in many of his other works. This style may simply have survived from earlier experiences in writing for newspapers, but it also serves to reinforce the impression that he regarded his works as a series with a unified mission.

Opening and closing statements in almost any of his works also reflect a unity of pattern. With his keen sense of territory, he began or ended most of them with a brief statement describing situation and ambience, while his books about people usually opened or closed with a reference to their "place" in history. "Ike Stockton is remotely associated with the Lincoln County War;" or "Golden, seventy-one miles southwest of Santa Fe, is in a setting befitting its name;" or "Miami is a hill city—rather a startling statement to make for the area of the Panhandle," he wrote in typical openings. In a fairly typical conclusion, one reads:

Neither Indian nor soldiers regretted leaving Fort Tulerosa. This was country for the dreamer and the poet. Beautiful beyond imagination. . .so serene, so calm, so thickly wooded and blanketed with varieties of mountain flowers and grasses. . .It is still a hunter's paradise. . .The mountain people here are kind and understand that a thing of beauty is a joy forever.[41]

This style at times makes one think of a series of guide books: "There are several roads that will take you to Inez;" "Most towns of New Mexico are conducive to healthy living. Take Fairview for instance;" or "[Manzano is] just the place for a businessman after a hard day's work."

F. Stanley may have intended this resemblance. His prefaces often reiterated his concern that reference sources, such as the Federal Writers' Project *American Guide Series,* frequently gave only a few lines to some places while omitting others altogether. Several times he listed among his "ghost works" a fifteen-volume set: "New Mexico Encyclopedia and Reference Guide, Volume I, A to Albuquerque."[42]

A certain fatalism, or heavy-hearted optimism, further characterized F. Stanley's style, again most noticeably in the place booklets. Few communities, for example, were so small or had lost so much population that he could not predict future growth while at the same time hinting at the opposite. Concerning Chilili he commented: "Places now mere villages may be the cities of the future. . .New Mexico has changed so completely in the last quarter of a century that no idea is far-fetched regarding it." Of Brilliant, the former Swastika, he observed: "With Kaiser Steel Corporation putting this area back in the coal business, it is possible that Brilliant may once again lift its head. Stranger things have happened." Of Capulín he wrote: "Even if all the school children are bused to Des Moines, and all church members go elsewhere to church, Capulin will survive." And of Grenville:

> With new cars and better pavement Grenville people do not mind driving to Raton to visit doctors or buy groceries and furniture. . .Whether Grenville will ever boom again is anybody's guess but it will be around for a while. Churches and school, garages, grocery store, post office, welding shop and the like will continue to function. The rest is in the hands of God.[43]

Another unifying factor in F. Stanley's works was his intense sense of mission. To paraphrase from several of the booklets, he wrote about communities that he believed to be "in danger of dying as did La Lande. . .Tabian and so many others. . .that once had promise." He wrote of farming communities such as Elida and Glenrio whose lifeblood of population had slowly drained away because their few small businesses could not compete with the increasing convenience of travel to bigger and better shopping centers. He wrote of mining towns that suddenly folded when their one industry shut down, leaving only empty sun-and-wind-whitened shells behind them; or of others that disappeared altogether, without leaving even a trace "to locate the site where the town once stood. No one knew definitely. Yet once it had its moment of glory. Sic transit."

In other words, whether they pertained to people, places or events, or whether they were "as much a part of . . .history as Coronado's visit," he believed many of his subjects to be in danger of passing into oblivion, "unless something is written about them—anything, not literary masterpieces—something in print. . .[so that] future generations may know and cherish the pioneering spirit of people who lived and had their being here."[44]

A corollary of F. Stanley's eagerness to get "something in print" about these mortal, regional subjects was his desire to present "the facts" or "the truth," unembellished by literary style or subjective analysis. "These are the facts," he wrote on more than one occasion: "I am not a novelist nor strictly attempting a biography, merely assembling the facts." Once, in a more jovial spirit, he said: "Sometimes the facts are so bare that the reader will wonder why I didn't put some clothes on them." And still another time:

> I am not looking for a place in the sun but for a place on the bookshelves of those who respect the truth and cherish it. Unembellished, it may not be a best seller, or even a seller at all, but we hope it may prove a definite contribution. . .[45]

If he could record "the truth," or enough facts, Father Stanley evidently felt that he might then succeed in preserving at least a portion of "the heritage of things that used to be." Very likely this eagerness lay at the heart of his formidable drive to deliver his stories in such great quantity.

Oh, I tell you, there's so many places yet to be written up, like San Cristobal, that people never heard of. . . I mean, where do you start? . . .Taos would take your whole lifetime. See, you've got Taos, Fernando de Taos, Ranchitos de Taos. . .I've got so many books planned ahead that I don't know if the good Lord is going to let me write them.[46]

Chapter Twelve

JUGGLING THE BOOKS

". . .a hundred interruptions a day"

F. Stanley frankly selected many of his topics according to the availability, or handiness, of archival resources. When he lived in Pep and Nazareth, Texas, for instance, eastern New Mexico was "you might say better off for it," because of his proximity to Roosevelt and Curry County courthouse files. During that period he turned out a booklet on almost every community in that area. On the other hand, the lack of *published* information likewise constituted an important factor. He often chose subjects, including people such as Joel Fowler, because he had found "material [about them] to be meager and scant to say the least." Occasionally, as in his series on outlaws, the topics he selected represented "a phase of her [New Mexico's] growth" or development that interested him and that he simply wanted to explore further.[47]

As time and his own funds permitted, he carried out extensive, and thorough, research. He traveled throughout New Mexico and west Texas, visiting localities that he thought he might write about. "I tried to make it a point to see what they looked like," he said. In each community he checked on the availability of documentary sources. Often he could find very little published information anywhere except in old newspaper files, and sometimes even these no longer existed. As he once said:

Some places. . .where do you get the records? There's nothing left of them. . .I know because I tried. Like with Tatum, I found two lines [published]. . .Same with Inez. What do they [libraries] have about Inez? What do they have on Watrous, on Tiptonville, on Lingo, Rogers?[48]

To supplement his information he sometimes interviewed old-timers, observing that "no two ever told the same tale alike." Occasionally these oral historians presented him with other difficulties.

> Now people are strange. As soon as they hear that you are writing about their grandfather, right away. . . they think you're out for business. If they only knew how much I still owe on a lot of—for instance on the Apache book I still owe eight hundred dollars.[49]

In his search for material, Father Stanley examined records written in both Spanish and English, some of them housed in museums, historical societies, libraries or stored in "other old corners where they keep files," such as attics, newspaper morgues and courthouse basements. Once or twice at closing time, he said, county clerks "almost came close to locking me in. . .but they called down because they saw the lights were on in the basement." Working with the older Spanish documents, he found, meant "reading some writing that looked more like chemical or electronic formulas than letters." Several times he traveled as far away as Los Angeles or Washington, D.C. Gathering material for *The Las Vegas Story (New Mexico)*, he estimated that he traveled "eighteen thousand, one hundred and forty-five miles to ascertain the facts."

Regardless of where he went, he filled spiral notebooks and stacks of yellow half-sheets with his scrawling hand-written notes. These he later filed in folders and boxes labeled with their subjects. When he had compiled all the information he needed, and found time to write, he organized his material into books or booklets.[50]

Finding time to write and do research required a certain amount of juggling. He always served his parishes with great zeal, and though the heaviest portion of his duties fell on Saturday and Sunday, a priest remains on call seven days a week, twenty-four hours a day. Usually Father Stanley's parishioners and bishop graciously recognized Monday as his day off, and he often used those days for short research trips. He could take up to two months per year in vacation time, and he used these periods for longer trips, financing travel expenses from his monthly stipend plus car allowance. Long trips also involved the trouble and expense of finding a substitute and reimbursing him. Father Stanley did most of his writing during lulls in parish work, piecing together paragraphs and pages in the midst of "the front and back doorbells, visits to hospitals, phone, people coming in for personal attention. . ." He accepted this as part of his job, but could not help regretting the many "sentences left in mid-air and lost forever because of a hundred interruptions a day."[51]

With each of his printers Father Stanley worked out an agreement covering the number of copies and the manner of payment.

> Here's the understanding we had; this is why a lot of publishers wouldn't touch me. The first printer I used was the World Press in Denver. The publisher was a Catholic, his name was Joe [Lou] Doughty. I said, "Now look Joe, I have no money. Would you be willing to risk with me that for any book I sell I would send you the money? In other words, I'll take nothing but I will be my own salesman, get rid of these books and that will pay your bill." And that's the understanding I had with anyone who has ever done a book for me, Pampa and Borger too.[52]

Father Stanley always "got rid" of his books, yet stayed perennially in debt to his printers. Actually his works sold rather quickly, mostly to individuals or libraries, but usually at little more than cost. Dealers often bought in bulk. They expected discounts and Father Stanley obliged by selling to them at prices lower than cost, which he established simply by dividing the printers' charges by the total number of copies run. He did not add in other expenses such as research trips, manuscript preparation, compilation of mailing lists, duplication of announcements, postage and incidentals. As he explained it:

> . . .now here's where the losses come in. Bookmen want forty percent discount. You can see that I have to un-

dersell these people. But they are the ones that buy most of them. I'll sell to Harvard and what do they want—one copy; or Texas University, one copy. These fellows [dealers] may take ten; that's forty percent loss on each that I will have to make up.[53]

While libraries accounted for a large part of his sales, few of them troubled to collect all of his works, at least not until recently—a factor that has contributed to their current scarcity. "Librarians," he once said,

> are very cagey about getting anything from me, because you see I publish my own works and sell as an individual. . .They say, "an individual—vanity press," so they don't bother and my flyer probably goes in file thirteen. Then later on when the Library of Congress lists it, or a brochure comes out [from an out-of-print dealer] with that item in it, then they want the book. By that time three or four hundred copies, or even five hundred are long gone. I usually give away a hundred and fifty at Christmas anyway.[54]

Although frustrated by the problems involved in producing and marketing his books, he entertained no personal animosity toward any individual dealer or librarian. On the contrary, he continually expressed gratitude to them for their unstinting assistance in his research. "Rare book dealers," he wrote in one of his prefaces, "form the phalanx that marches at the head of the column of ever broadening knowledge of the Southwest and its history." And he noted that there is, or should be, "a feeling of kinship when books are the common denominator, among those who handle books, work with books and attempt—like myself—to produce books."[55]

With few exceptions, all of F. Stanley's books or booklets were limited to a press run of four or five hundred copies, because "John Lipsey, a dealer in Colorado Springs," suggested that "psychologically the limitation note would induce people to buy." The known exceptions are *The Grant That Maxwell Bought,* which he limited to two hundred and fifty copies "because they said it wouldn't sell," and *Des-*

peradoes of New Mexico, which had a press run of eight hundred copies.[56] He rarely reissued any of his books, two known exceptions being *Jim Courtright* and *Socorro: The Oasis,* for if he did so he reduced their value to dealers, particularly out-of-print specialists. "I always said in the folder they wouldn't be reprinted because, after we reprint, the price on the original goes down." But, of course, these inflated out-of-print prices usually by-passed F. Stanley's pocket.[57]

Father Stanley used Denver's World Press until around 1960, when he began taking his work to Pampa Print Shop, Jim Hess Printers in Borger, and possibly other unidentified jobbers in Pep, Nazareth, Dumas, and Pantex, Texas —the places of publication given in his booklets. For some reason he never used a New Mexico press. Regarding his switch to Texas printers, he explained:

> He [World Press] got so exorbitant; if I didn't sell a book for ten or twelve dollars I couldn't pay him. Well who would pay ten or twelve dollars for a book when you could buy a paperback for a quarter? . . .I mean figuratively, at that time, twenty years ago when I started.
>
> You take the Raton book; it sold for a dollar and a half. Now [1969] some dealers have a fairly good copy for fifty dollars. Like one dealer in Colorado Springs told me, "Don't die! I'm making money off of you." And there's one book dealer in Oklahoma City that gets fifteen dollars a copy on all those little booklets once they get out of print—fifteen dollars a copy! And here I sit, trying to figure out how they can be sold so I'll be able to get the next batch out.[58]

Chapter Thirteen

CRITICAL RECEPTION

". . .you develop this fear complex"

While the reasons may be understandable, one of the ironies in Father Stanley's career as a writer is that he did so much, yet profited so little from his contributions in any sense. Any money he made from sales he plowed back into the business so to speak, and while he always hoped that one of the colleges or universities in New Mexico or Texas would award him an honorary degree, "So far nobody's ever offered." Said Father Stanley:

> Where was it somebody wrote that the reason why God didn't give us larger hands was so we couldn't pat ourselves on the back? Well, he succeeded very well indeed. See, it's for other people to pat you on the back. That's why I hope someday that Eastern New Mexico or the University of New Mexico, or Las Cruces, or Highlands could—just to make me feel I'm not wasting my time—say, "Well, all right. We're going to give you an honorary *some*thing, like a sheepskin of some sort, because of what you did for New Mexico."[59]

The unavoidable problem in assessing F. Stanley's contributions is that, as a writer and a historian, he deserves both praise and blame. He seems to have reaped mostly the latter, mainly in the form of silent rejection; very little open reaction to his work exists. Much of the negative criticism has been, in effect, "whispered," as for example a rumor that circulated several years ago alleging that the oil companies hired him as a propagandist, and that he earned his commissions by writing *The Early Days of the Oil Industry in the Texas Panhandle* plus the booklets on Skellytown, Phillips and so forth.

Another rumor, still current, has it that he hired or

assigned younger priests to do his research, particularly to interview old-timers in out-of-the-way places. F. Stanley knew about the first allegation, attributing it to rising gasoline prices and "the lines people were forming to get a couple of gallons; you know how people act when they get frustrated." He did not refer to the second rumor, but it seems unlikely too. In the first place, Father Stanley always seemed to enjoy doing research. In the second place, he lacked both the money, and the authority within the Church hierarchy, to make it feasible for him to farm this type of work out to anyone else, certainly not as a regular practice. Had he done so, however, he would not have been the first. Other historians have hired assistants to collect notes for them, even sometimes to help compile the final results, an extreme example being Hubert Howe Bancroft. And of course F. Stanley once gave this sort of assistance himself when he helped gather notes for *Our Catholic Heritage in Texas*. Of interest here too is his dedication of *Rodeo Town* to "T. A. Vigil, whose untiring efforts in research and notetaking made this book possible."[60]

Rumors and whispers, however, probably would not have hurt F. Stanley's reputation had it not been for the lack of recognition given him by the scholarly community. Disregarding the fact that hundreds of people bought and presumably read his books, almost invariably they met with indifference from scholars. Reviewers rarely mentioned them, professional historians rarely cited them, bibliographers rarely listed them and, as noted, librarians often did not bother to collect them all.

But as with all rules, this one had some notable exceptions. In his *Guide to Life and Literature of the Southwest*, J. Frank Dobie described *The Grant That Maxwell Bought* as "perhaps stronger on characters involved during the long litigation over the land, and containing more documentary evidence," than William Keleher's *Maxwell Land Grant: A New Mexico Item*. In *The Booklover's Southwest*, Walter S. Campbell (Stanley Vestal) mentioned *Desperadoes of New Mexico*, calling it "interesting, readable, valuable," though he did not fail to point out that it included "some

54

fables about Billy the Kid." Even more briefly, in *The Santa Fe Trail*, Jack Rittenhouse cited *Fort Union* as "the first book-length work on the history" of that post. Then, in 1964, with a long and well-documented attack that he published in *Burs Under the Saddle: A Second Look at Books and Histories of the West*, Ramon Adams wiped out any encouragement that F. Stanley might have derived from these, or any other, small bits of praise.[61]

Adams' attack had considerable impact, at least in Father Stanley's estimation. He tried to joke about it, but found it hard to maintain a philosophical attitude. "Do you know," he said, "that a dealer refused to sell me a copy because he thought I'd go out and commit suicide after that man got through with me?" And he added,

> You would like once, just once, to get some recognition . . .For instance I had four chapters finished on Portales at one point, but—you develop this fear complex. And it has hurt me; a lot of people have cancelled [standing orders] because of all this.[62]

"Just as burs under the saddle irritate a horse," Adams explained in the preface of his book, "so the constant writing of inaccurate history irritates the historian." The ten-page section that he devoted to F. Stanley concentrated on an analysis of six works: *The Antonchico, New Mexico Story; Jim Courtright: Two Gun Marshal of Fort Worth; Desperadoes of New Mexico; No Tears for Black Jack* [*sic*]; *Dave Rudabaugh: Border Ruffian;* and *The Shakespeare, New Mexico Story*. The last named item Adams cited as printed in Panten [*sic*] Texas, which, with his transcriptions of some other titles, showed him capable of a few careless mistakes of his own.[63]

Adams devoted only two paragraphs each to the Antonchico and Shakespeare booklets, noting that "Father Stanley has written a great many pamphlets on various places, but only a few will be listed here [Adams mentioned two]. All of them are difficult to read, paragraphs sometimes running on for three or more pages and including various unrelated subjects."

The other four books Adams analyzed in greater detail. He pointed out quantities of small, careless errors, such as a reference in *Desperadoes of New Mexico* to "James W. Ball named 'John,' a mistake he [F. Stanley] should have caught himself." He quoted passage after passage from their pages, refuting facts, differing with interpretations, citing "ridiculous assumptions, unsubstantiated opinions, insufficient evidence, contradictions, and omissions." Several times he called attention to what he termed F. Stanley's "weakness for quoting from undependable sources," adding asides such as "one should be well enough acquainted with his subject to know which accounts to reject," or "It is hard to understand why anyone trying to write history would quote accounts which he must know are inaccurate." Adams concluded his analysis of *Dave Rudabaugh* with the observation that "Again, as in most of his other works, the excessively long paragraphs, filled with unrelated material, are irritating to the reader."[64]

Adams was, to some extent, correct. Defects do mar and weaken F. Stanley's work, bibliographically, historically and stylistically. A casual browser quickly encounters obvious flaws such as incomplete or puzzling citations, typographical errors, even embarrassingly faulty sentences here and there. A more careful reading reveals factual mistakes, a scissors-and-tape quality to some of the writing, and other evidence of hasty proofreading and revision. Long, unassimilated quotations make some of the works difficult to read.

On occasion he altered the facts in his material to shield others or possibly to avoid difficulties for himself. In *Desperadoes* he changed outlaw Port Stockton's name to Porter Stogden to keep from offending a prominent family, and in *The Grant That Maxwell Bought* he omitted mention of an illegitimate son for similar reasons. But however kind his motives, the presence of errors such as these affected his credibility. As he once lamented:

people write to me and say, "You don't know your history." I know my history. I've been working long enough, and going to the primary sources. I don't know where else to go. . .Because where do you go? You go to the government documents, you go to letters. And when you go to letters people start suing you. . .So you have to take a lot of—take a beating with a lot of the work you do.[65]

Most of F. Stanley's books and some of his booklets include bibliographies, though in the booklets these usually take the form of abbreviated reading lists. Only the first two, *Raton Chronicle* and *One Half Mile From Heaven*, have formal endnotes. In *The Civil War in New Mexico*, he gathered rather discoursive "Notes and Comments" at ends of chapters. In most of his other works he inserted brief source notes in parentheses at the ends of sentences or paragraphs, often using a puzzling abbreviation of his own invention which he nowhere formally explained: (o.c.). When asked, he replied that this stands for *op. cit.* The term in itself is an abbreviation for *opere citato*, "in the work cited," and is easily confused with *loc. cit.* or *ibid.* Most writers now avoid it altogether, but F. Stanley liked it, shortened it still further, thus conserving space, and used it in place of all three terms.

That he worried about conserving space, even the space occupied by one or two letters, probably accounts not only for the "paragraphs sometimes running on for three or more pages and including various unrelated subjects" that Adams complained about. Paragraph indentations obviously take up space, as does documentation. To cut costs, F. Stanley kept both to an absolute minimum. He went even further, sacrificing space in his forewords by arguing repeatedly against the scholarly convention of providing any citations at all. He also worried about the amount of time that it takes to prepare footnotes.

Now *Raton Chronicle* does have footnotes, the Cimarron book has footnotes. But then I figured that it took so much longer; because the copy comes back, then you go over it, then the printer has to get in the footnote material, and all. And it was such a headache. . .[66]

In *The Clayton (New Mexico) Story*, one of his earliest works, he wrote: "Books, records, archives, newspapers out of print or hard to find are not listed, because students and research-scholars know where to find them; others wouldn't be interested. . ." In *The Jicarilla Apaches* he put it this way:

> Once again the age old debate came up. Should there or should there not be footnotes. Again we felt justified in placing what might normally have been footnotes next to the text. This for several reasons. Most people find footnotes a bother. Those who have made a study of Indians really do not need them. They know where the sources are. . .Footnotes really do not tell anymore than what the author just got through saying. . .Time is the test of a man's research.[67]

And in *The Odyssey of Juan Archibeque* he asserted:

> Rather than annoy the reader with little numbers after certain references. . .take my word for it that the facts are gleaned from the Archives of the Indies, the works of Hodge, Hackett, Fray Angelico, Castañeda, the reports of the Audiencia, Santa Fe Archives, New Mexico Archives.[68]

While a researcher might, incidentally, have difficulty in identifying "the Santa Fe Archives" (that unique little city has several such repositories, including the Archdiocese of Santa Fe, the State Records Center and Archives, the Museum of New Mexico and the New Mexico State Library), F. Stanley undoubtedly did "glean the facts" from all of the resources mentioned above, and more. As he also reminded his readers many times, in conducting his own studies he always went to the primary sources, gathering some valuable, difficult to locate or translate, documentary material along the way.

On the other hand, running in counterpoint to F. Stanley's attitude toward documentation was his equally often expressed hope that the material he gathered would serve as "a basis, something for future students to look into to get a start, a footing that will increase their knowledge of the Land of Enchantment, its cities, towns and people." He emphasized this point as forcefully and frequently as he denied the necessity for documentation. "But I try to make everything primary as a basis for research students," he explained. "That's why everything in the books was not written, let's say, as a novelist would write it, but as a research student would write. Fact! This is it, pure and simple, no diluting. Here it all is. And I hope until the day I die that they are that much ahead." And in one of his prefaces he wrote: "I hope they [southwesterners] at least say a prayer for me, gathering as I have, compiling as I did over the years, so much of the history of their fore-fathers."[69]

Among the most dismaying flaws in F. Stanley's work are the lack of selectivity and of synthesis in his use of quoted material. As Adams emphasized, he did not seem to weigh the credibility of his sources. Because F. Stanley himself enjoyed a good tale, he may have knowingly mixed a fable or two into his tincture of "fact pure and simple." Other historians have done this and gotten away with it (for example Carl Sandburg, who used the questionable Ann Rutledge story in his biography of Lincoln), but they had extraordinary literary or analytical skills which compensated for any errors of a major or minor nature. F. Stanley made no pretenses as a literary artist or analytical historian. He knew his material, had in fact steeped himself in it, and possessed considerable perspective. He also knew how to tell a good story, and while he denied writing "as a novelist," sometimes he did. Nevertheless, on occasion, he not only trusted unreliable accounts, he also quoted long passages from them, relying on these to carry his narrative along. He discussed this practice, as he did his other faults, in many prefaces. In *Jim Courtright* we read:

> Newspaper accounts are followed verbatim. Why? For several reasons. To prove that we do not have to em-bellish; to state the facts; to give the news as it hap-pened in Courtright's day, not as we. . .accepted another's word for it.[70]

F. Stanley most noticeably resorted to lengthy quotations in his place booklets, making his selections more or less at random and using them to capture the tone or personality of a community over a period of years. Contrary to Adams' assumption, he did not always do this. In some of the booklets, however, and even in some of the longer works, lists of characters in a play, or of visitors from out of town, or verbatim accounts of social events suddenly appear after a few pages of general narrative, with only a brief transitional phrase (or none at all) to explain their presence to the reader. The effect could be startling. The following excerpts from *The Gladstone New Mexico Story*, pages five through twenty-two, may illustrate the point. The quotation marks and o.c. notations are F. Stanley's.

Continuing with quotes through the years we get a fair picture of life as it was and is lived at Gladstone. "Brother Owen of the Methodist Church filled his regular appointment Sunday. . .The honor roll for the Gladstone school is as follows: Susie Bada, Jim Page, Paul Richey, Billy Tom Richey, Glen Jones, Bertha Richey." (o.c. Jan. 1929).

.   .   .   .

An eight pound baby girl arrived at the home of Mr. and Mrs. Cloyd Rigdon Friday. . .Earl Kephart helped M. A. Spurgeon overhaul his tractor Tuesday. . .The Santa Fe asked to abandon its railroad at Capulin and Desmoines [*sic*] March, 1935. (May 30). . .The bean threashers [*sic*] have been busy in our community this week. . .The Women's Home Demonstration Club met with Will Luellen last Wednesday. The club quilted out a quilt and Mrs. Coldwell showed them how to make a flag trap and a shower bath. . .Sunday School is picking up some; we notice the presence of some Sunday that have not been there for quite a while due to illness.

.   .   .   .

1957—"Mrs. Ralph Bryan, Helen and Ricky were hostesses and host to a weiner roast at their home Saturday night. . .A family reunion was held at the Aubrey Baker home August 14." (o.c.)

.   .   .   .

Mrs. Bob Maness has been in the hospital at Clayton
all this past week. . .Donald Kuhlman is spending two
weeks with Mr. and Mrs. Aladar Bada while his mother
is in the process of moving to Colorado Springs." (o.c.
May 25, 1966).[71]

The words "Colorado Springs" and the source note conclude
the Gladstone story. It was one of his last booklets on New
Mexico. Six years earlier, explaining the "roll calls" of obscure people, he wrote:

People make up a city. . .and where people contributed to the history of the city their names appear.
This explains why the author uses so many quotes in
all his books. . .While he is more apt to be known as
a recorder than a writer, he is willing to take that risk
and leaving the writing to another generation, when
Clovis takes on the color of antiquity as experienced
by Santa Fe, Belen, Socorro, Taos and other ancients
of the Land of Enchantment [sic].[72]

Father Stanley, in other words, not only hunted for
"primary" resource material, he also tried to record and
present the essence of this material in its purest form, un-
corrupted by "secondary" opinion or commentary. In a
sense he was searching for gold, not as an earthly but an
alchemical element, and not for himself but as a gift to
his readers. It was a task of mythical proportions which,
as he understood it, left him little time to spare for revis-
ing or proofreading. The faulty syntax in the last sentence
of the quotation above no doubt resulted from the tremen-
dous pressure that he imposed upon himself to turn out
works in quantity, to attempt alone a Herculean labor that
needed at least a hundred times the manpower. That same
year, 1966, he published fourteen titles, including the full-
length book on Clovis in which those lines appeared.

Even the most hastily written of F. Stanley's books
offers something of value to the reader. The titles alone
are reminders of the "Brigadoons" of New Mexico, with
their pretty or evocative names like Alma, Hermosa, Villanueva, Questa, La Lande; or of small, sturdy places with

"those resounding Western names that whet the historical appetite," like Milnesand or Plemons.[73] The information they present within their blue or golden covers can of course be found elsewhere if one is prepared to travel some distance and then spend hours delving in archives, glaring back at microfilm, perhaps translating some Cervantean Spanish, or leafing through dusty, crumbling files in out-of-the-way courthouse basements. But without F. Stanley's efforts, it would have remained virtually inaccessible for most people.

Although he did not spend much time polishing his prose, some of his passages sparkle with fine writing, an appealing humor, or interesting insights. One may open any of his works at random and find plenty of examples comparable to these:

> Sit down on the banks of the ever flowing Cimarron. Let the wind speak. It has a hundred voices that bewitch as the sun bakes and the river enchants. . .You settle back and your story is born.

> You can see more of less and love it better than all the sights of a county fair.

> Fortunately for the Apaches they had no gold. . .no pueblo, no written record of the past, no cook book. It was because they had none of these things that they survived.

> Satanta will not be found among the greats, only with the near-greats. But even the near-greats have some message.

> Oil was the district judge pronouncing sentence on which towns should live, which die, or glow with fame and glory for a time then fade into the background. It was also the magician bringing life out of the void.

> Not in twenty lifetimes can any one individual ever get to know all there is to know about New Mexico and its hidden pathways to the past.

The few landmarks Chapman saw in 1916 are all gone.
The silence that is New Mexico remains.

.   .   .   .

The past is history; the present activity.[74]

Chapter Fourteen

A MAN'S REACH

"Take him for what he is worth"

It is difficult to say to what extent negative criticism and neglect may have personally affected Father Stanley. Some of his works in the 1970s showed considerable care in preparation, but no more so than his major efforts in earlier decades. He knew his own limitations as well as any of his critics did, but he believed quite sincerely that the flaws in his work were largely literary in nature and therefore of little overall significance; or alternatively that they represented realities over which he had little control, such as his limited time or the cost of typesetting footnotes. His first reactions may be surmised from comments in the foreword to *Dave Rudabaugh.*

> I used to apologize for my mistakes. Come to think of it, why should I? I tried; that's more than my critics did. I investigated to the best of my ability, often going sleepless and hungry in order to attain the facts. No patron has come along the way. I had to rough it alone. . .The book may not be literary, but it is factual. In the long run, truth survives.[75]

Two years later, in *The Duke City,* he confessed from a somewhat different perspective: "I am grateful for all criticism—constructive or otherwise." And in *Satanta and the Kiowas,* 1968, he pled: "Let my mistakes be my Calvary, and let my readers be my confessors from whom we hope to obtain pardon and forgiveness."[76]

Simply and with a kind of humble determination, he persevered for many years, his principal resources being his formidable drive and his eagerness to help preserve the history of the region he loved so well. No doubt he attempted too much; probably, as with so many of us, his

reach exceeded his grasp. His hope, which he stated over
and over again, was that his books would provide guidance
for others and "prove a. . .contribution to Western Americana."[77] That purpose and his dedication to it do not deserve to be lightly dismissed.

Taken as a whole, with all its human flaws, F. Stanley's work stands as a unique contribution, as much a part
of the written record "as Coronado's visit." Even Ramon
Adams acknowledged that "he deserves a full measure of
credit for supplying hitherto unpublished information," for
putting something into print about obscure places and people, for adding to the body of recorded knowledge about
the Southwest. Whatever the final evaluation may be, however, it is certain that F. Stanley has earned a place in
southwestern history in his own right.[78]

AN F. STANLEY BIBLIOGRAPHY

The bibliography that follows provides essentially un-annotated citations of all known published books and booklets by F. Stanley. It does not include any of his articles or unpublished manuscripts; it also omits essays about him and reviews of his works by other writers. With the exception of some of the dust jackets, it is based on examination of volumes in the Father Stanley Crocchiola Collection in Golden Library of Eastern New Mexico University, Portales.

The bibliography is arranged alphabetically by title in letter-by-letter, rather than word-by-word, order, as spelled, disregarding initial articles. (Titles such as *The Los Alamos, New Mexico Story* are, however, entered under the second article.) Each entry describes distinguishing physical features, and records complete title, place and date of publication, printer when known, and pagination. The form and order in which these items appear within entries corresponds as closely as possible to that found in the works themselves, except that title variations are noted toward the end of each entry and limitation notes are placed after imprint. Punctuation is added sparingly to F. Stanley's.

The author's works share a number of physical characteristics. In addition to a certain uniformity of color among their covers, described elsewhere, all of the booklets measure approximately 5½ by 8½ inches, and consist of one saddle-stitched (stapled) signature. Title pages in the earlier New Mexico booklets were decorated with two, five-pointed stars; one star in the space separating author from title, the other between title and imprint. Covers of New Mexico booklets also display a Zia symbol, printed in red, in the lower left front corner until 1966, and after that date, usually in center front. These later volumes often had three small, horizontally-centered squares embellishing their title pages, instead of the two stars.

Texas booklets featured the motif of three squares centered on either their covers or title pages, and occasionally on both.[79]

F. Stanley counted the title pages of his booklets as page one, regardless of whether a folio was actually printed there, and always listed his post office box number as part of the imprint, with month as well as year of publication. For some reason, he omitted the names of printers in his booklets, but, with the exception of *Fort Union (New Mexico)*, his longer works always included printers' names, usually on title page versos. He routinely autographed his works unless requested not to do so; unsigned copies are scarce. For the sake of brevity, the bibliography omits reference to these standard characteristics.

Several of the Stanley booklets and one or two of the books provided no publication clues at all. Information pertaining to these has been based on Library of Congress catalog entries, preceded in our bibliography by the notation "LC"—for example, "[LC: White Deer, Texas, 1960]." Actually, White Deer seems an unlikely place of publication, probably derived by LC from a foreword in *The San Marcial (New Mexico) Story* datelined "White Deer, Texas, May 31, 1960." Evidence, in works with both title pages as well as datelines, suggests that during his term there Father Stanley took his work to printers in other places; White Deer probably had no printer.

In recording titles, entries in the bibliography do not tamper with spelling. For instance, the second volume of the three volume set, *Ciudad Santa Fe*, carried a typographical error. Its title page, cover and dust jacket spelled the first word *Cuidad* which, amusingly, resembles "careful" in Spanish.[80] The printer pasted corrective labels over the error in each spot on most copies, but the volume in Golden Library escaped this treatment. F. Stanley consistently misspelled Tularosa, substituting an "e" for the first "a."

As for other titles, F. Stanley typically used parentheses on covers and commas on title pages to set apart names of states. Captions at the head of the first page of text frequently omitted state names altogether. Titles on dust jackets sometimes varied from those appearing on front covers, spines, title pages or in captions. The bibliography notes these variations. The notation, "Cover title ( )," at the end of many booklet entries, is an arbitrary note that stands for F. Stanley"s typical cover title style when this varied from the title shown on the title page. The absence of this notation indicates that he used the same form and punctuation on both title page and cover.

In recording pagination all numbers in brackets indicate unnumbered pages, generally blank, although some preliminary pages may carry printing. An entry such as "[i-iv] i-x 1-221 [222]" indicates that the book has four unnumbered pages and ten preliminary pages with Roman folios, and that it has 221 pages of text with Arabic folios beginning with numbered page 1, followed by a blank page [222].

An entry such as "1 [2] 3-22, b*l*" means that the booklet described begins with a title page numbered one, followed by a blank verso [2], with text beginning on numbered page three and concluding at numbered page twenty-two, followed in turn by a blank leaf which forms an integral part of the gathering.

Blank, and other unnumbered leaves or pages occurring between chapters, are disregarded. The bibliography does, however, record the number and style of illustrations, using the term "print" for those printed on one side of a leaf and "plate" for any inserted into a gathering.

The Boston Public Library owns an apparently unique set of the booklets bound in six volumes and labeled "New Mexico Community Pamphlets by Father Stanley." The BPL has no record of where or when it obtained the set. Each volume consists of fourteen booklets, in their original bright paper covers, arranged in approximately sequential order by time of publication. Volume I, 1960-62, has a printed title page, table of contents, and a preface, the latter being simply a copy of the foreword to *The San Marcial (New Mexico) Story. The National Union Catalog, 1973-1977* carried an entry for the set, but subsequent editions dropped it, and it does not appear in the OCLC data base. The 1973-77 NUC entry attributed ownership solely to the Boston Public Library. Anyone familiar with F. Stanley's works will question the form in which his name appears on the title page of the set, and the use of the term "pamphlet" there. "It seems," says Laura V. Monti, Keeper of Rare Books and Manuscripts at BPL, "that the original owner had the pamphlets bound uniformly with what appears to be a specially printed title-page for each volume."[81]

Very likely all of the clothbound volumes originally had dust jackets, with the possible exception of *The Grant That Maxwell Bought*. Jackets on the Texas volumes varied considerably, but those on the New Mexico volumes were quite similar to one another. Resembling the books that they covered, they were golden-yellow with red lettering. Some also displayed the Zia symbol, printed in red in the lower left front corner. The bibliography describes only those jackets that differed significantly from the usual, and merely notes the presence of others with the words "dust jacket."

BOOKS AND BOOKLETS

BY

F. STANLEY

(1) *The Abiquiu (New Mexico) Story* [cover title]. [LC: White Deer, Texas, 1960]. [1]-35 [36]. "References and Helps for Further Study," 35. Head of text, "Abiquiu, New Mexico Story."

(2) *The Abo, New Mexico Story.* Pep, Texas, June, 1966. (Limited to 400 Copies). [1] 2-20. Cover title ( ).

(3) *The Acoma, New Mexico Story.* Pep, Texas, May, 1963. (Limited to 500 Copies). 1 2-24. Cover title ( ).

(4) *The Alamogordo, New Mexico Story.* Pep, Texas, August, 1963. (Limited to 500 Copies). 1 2-20. Cover title ( ).

(5) *The Alma (New Mexico) Story* [cover title]. [LC: White Deer, Texas, 1960]. [1] 2-18, b*l.* "Suggested Reading," 18. Head of text, "The Alma, N. Mexico Story."

(6) *The Antonchico (New Mexico) Story* [cover title]. [LC: White Deer, Texas, 1960]. [1] 2-18, b*l.* "Suggested Reading—Available Material," 18. Head of text, "Antonchico, N. Mexico Story."

(7) *The Apaches of New Mexico: 1540-1940.* [Pampa, Texas: Pampa Print Shop, 1962]. [i-ii] i-v [vi-vii] 1-449. "Foreword," i-iv, datelined "St. Francis—Pantex, Texas, October 31, 1961." "Bibliography and Sources," 425-438. "Index," 434-449. Cloth, golden-yellow lettered in red. Dust jacket.

(8) *The Arch New Mexico Story.* Pep, Texas, February, 1967. (Limited to 400 Copies). 1 2-22, b*l.* Cover title ( ).

(9) *The Baldy (New Mexico) Story.* Nazareth, Texas, November, 1973. (Limited to 400 Copies). 1 2-20. Head of text, "The Baldy Story."

(10) *The Belen, New Mexico Story.* Pantex, Texas, July, 1962. (Limited to 500 Copies). 1 [2] 3-20. Cover title ( ).

(11) *The Bernalillo, New Mexico Story.* Pep, Texas, August, 1964. (Limited to 400 Copies). 1 2-20. Cover title ( ).

(12) *The Bethel, New Mexico Story.* Pep, Texas, August, 1966. (Limited to 400 Copies). 1 2-20. Cover title ( ).

(13) *The Black Tower, New Mexico Story.* Pep, Texas, January, 1969. (Limited to 400 Copies). 1 2-20. Head of text, "The Black Tower Story." Cover title ( ).

(14) *The Bland, New Mexico Story.* Pep, Texas, March, 1964. (Limited to 400 Copies). 1 [2] 3-20. Cover title ( ).

(15) *The Blossburg, New Mexico Story.* Pantex, Texas, March, 1962. 1 2-20. Cover title ( ).

(16) *The Brilliant, New Mexico Story.* Pep, Texas, January, 1967. (Limited to 400 Copies). [1-2] 3-26, b*l.* Illus: 4 prints. Cover title ( ).

(17) *The Canadian Texas Story.* Nazareth, Texas, January, 1975. (Limited to 400 Copies). 1 2-19 [20]. Head of text, "The Canadian Story."

(18) *The Capulin New Mexico Story.* Nazareth, Texas, December, 1970. (Limited to 400 Copies). 1 2-24. Head of text, "The Capulin Story." Cover title ( ).

(19) *The Carbonateville, New Mexico Story.* Pep, Texas, April, 1966. (Limited to 400 Copies). 1 2-20. Cover title ( ).

(20) *The Carlsbad, New Mexico Story.* Pep, Texas, July,

1963. (Limited to 500 Copies). 1 [2] 3-20. Cover
title ( ).

(21) *The Catskill, New Mexico Story.* Pep, Texas, February, 1964. (Limited to 400 Copies). 1 [2] 3-20. Illus:
1 print. Cover title ( ).

(22) *The Causey, New Mexico Story.* Pep, Texas, August,
1966. (Limited to 400 Copies). 1 2-20. Cover title ( ).

(23) *The Cerrillos, New Mexico Story.* Pep, Texas, April,
1964. (Limited to 400 Copies). 1 [2] 3-20. Cover
title ( ).

(24) *The Channing Texas Story.* Nazareth, Texas, August, 1974. (Limited to 400 Copies). 1 2-22, b*l.*

(25) *The Chilili, New Mexico Story.* Pep, Texas, June,
1966. (Limited to 400 Copies). 1 2-20. Cover title ( ).

(26) *The Chloride, New Mexico Story.* Pantex, Texas,
March, 1962. 1 2-20. Cover title ( ).

Chimayó—See *Potrero de Chimayo.*

(27) *Ciudad Santa Fe:* [Vol. I] *Spanish Domination:
1610-1821.* [Denver: The World Press, Inc., 1958].
[i-v] vi-ix [x] 1-412. "Dedication [to]. . .T. A.
Vigil, who helped to translate ancient documents; . . .
the Bishop of Amarillo, who placed his valuable archives at my disposal; the rector of Montezuma Seminary for further use of the Archives of the Indies
. . . ." [v]. "Foreword A," viii, datelined "Canadian,
Texas, August 16, 1954." "Bibliography," 405-412.
Spine and preliminary page [i], "Ciudad Santa Fe:
Spanish Domination (1610-1821)." Cloth, golden-
yellow lettered in red. Dust jacket.

(28) *Cuidad* [sic] *Santa Fe: Volume II: Mexican Rule:
1821-1846.* [Pampa, Texas: Pampa Print Shop,
1962]. —Limited to 500 Copies—. [i-iii] i-v 1-302.
"Foreword," i-iii, datelined "Pantex (St. Francis
Village), Texas, June 4, 1962." "Bibliography," 277-

285. "Index," 287-302. Cloth, golden-yellow lettered in red. Dust jacket.

(29) *Ciudad Santa Fe:* [Vol. III] *Territorial Days: 1846-1912.* [Pampa, Texas: Pampa Print Shop, 1965]. —Limited to 500 Copies—. [i-iii] i-v [vi-vii] 1-300, b*l.* "Foreword," [i]-v, datelined "Pep, Texas, February 8, 1965." "Bibliography," 289-297. "Index," 299-310. Cloth, golden-yellow lettered in red. Dust jacket.

(30) *The Civil War in New Mexico.* [Denver: The World Press, Inc., 1960]. [i-vi] vii-xiii [xiv-xvi] 1-508, b*l.* "Dedicated to the New Mexico Volunteers Who Deserve a Bigger Monumeut Than I Can Build," v. "Foreword," ix-xiii, datelined "White Deer, Texas, December 31, 1959." "A Bibliography," 503-508. Cloth, golden-yellow lettered in red. Dust jacket.

(31) *Clay Allison.* [Denver: World Press, Inc., 1956]. [i-viii] ix-xi [xii] 1-236. "Dedication to the memory of the late Earl VanDale of Amarillo, Texas who had hoped to live long enough to write the story of Clay Allison," v. "Foreword," ix-xi. "Bibliography," 229-236. Cloth, golden-yellow lettered in red. Dust jacket.

(32) *The Clayton (New Mexico) Story* [cover title]. [LC: White Deer, Texas, 1960]. [1]-42, b*l.* "Suggested Reading," 42. Head of text, "Clayton, New Mexico Story."

(33) *The Clovis, New Mexico, Story.* [Pampa, Texas: Pampa Print Shop, 1966]. —Limited to 500 Copies—. [i-v] i-x [xi-xii] 1-358. "Foreword," i-x. "Bibliography," 329-334. "Index," 335-358. Cloth, yellow lettered in red. Dust jacket.

(34) *The Colfax, New Mexico Story.* Pep, Texas, January, 1967. (Limited to 400 Copies). 1 2-20. Cover title ( ).

(35) *The Colmor, New Mexico Story.* Pep, Texas, Janu-

ary, 1967. (Limited to 400 Copies). 1 2-20. Cover title ( ).

(36) *The Columbus, New Mexico Story.* Pep, Texas, February, 1966. (Limited to 400 Copies). 1 [2] 3-22, b*l.* Cover title ( ).

Cuidad Santa Fe—See *Ciudad Santa Fe, Volume II.*

(37) *The Dalhart Texas Story.* Nazareth, Texas, January, 1975. (Limited to 400 Copies). [1] 2-19 [20]. Head of text, "The Dalhart Story."

(38) *Dave Rudabaugh: Border Ruffian.* [Denver: World Press, Inc., 1961]. [i-iv] vi-viii 1-200. Illus: 6 plates. "Foreword," vi-viii, datelined "October 31, 1960, Dumas, Texas." "Bibliography," 197-200. Cloth. golden-yellow lettered in red. Dust jacket.

(39) *The Dawson, New Mexico Story.* Pantex, Texas, September, 1961. 1 [2] 3-20. Cover title ( ).

(40) *The Dawson Tragedies.* Pep, Texas, December, 1965. (Limited to 400 Copies). 1 2-20. Cover title ( ).

(41) *The Deming, New Mexico Story.* Pantex, Texas, October, 1963. Limited to 500 Copies. 1 [2] 3-20. Cover title ( ).

(42) *The Des Moines, New Mexico Story.* Pep, Texas, June, 1965. (Limited to 400 Copies) 1 2-20. Cover title ( ).

(43) *Desperadoes of New Mexico.* [Denver: The World Press, Inc., 1953. "Limited Edition of New Mexico Desperadoes. This Book Number. . .of an edition limited to 800 volumes."] [i-vi] vii-xv [xvi] 1-320. Illus: 16 plates. "Dedication To the little known frontier marshals of New Mexico who helped make the Land of Enchantment a better place to live in," [vi]. "Foreword," ix-xv, datelined "Canadian, Texas —January 3, 1953." "Bibliography," 317-320. Cloth, golden-yellow lettered in red. Dust jacket.

(44) *The Dora, New Mexico Story.* Pep, Texas, January, 1967. (Limited to 400 Copies). 1 [2] 3-23 [24]. Cover title ( ).

(45) *The Duke City: The Story of Albuquerque, New Mexico: 1706-1956.* [Pampa, Texas: Pampa Print Shop, 1963]. [i-vi] i-xii [xiv] 1-267 [268]. "Foreword," i-xii. "Bibliography," 235-249. "Index," 251-267. Title on preliminary page [i], "The Duke City." Cloth, yellow lettered in red. Dust jacket.

(46) *The Eagle Nest New Mexico Story.* Nazareth, Texas, January, 1973. (Limited to 400 Copies). 1 [2], 3-22, b*l*. Head of text, "The Eagle Nest Story." Cover title ( ).

(47) *The Early Days of the Oil Industry in the Texas Panhandle: 1919-1929.* [Borger, Texas: Hess Publishing Co., 1973]. [i-iv] i-iv [v-vii] 1-414. "Foreword," i-iv, datelined "Nazareth, Texas, February 8, 1973." "Bibliography," 387-394. [Index] 395-414. Cloth, turquoise-green lettered in black. Dust jacket: white background lettered in turquoise.

(48) *The Elida, New Mexico Story.* Pep, Texas, March, 1966. (Limited to 400 Copies). 1 [2] 3-22, b*l*. Head of text, "The Elida, New Mexico, Story." Cover title ( ).

(49) *The Elizabethtown, New Mexico Story.* Dumas, Texas, March, 1961. 1 [2] 3-19 [20]. "Bibliography," 19. Cover title ( ).

(50) *The Estelline Texas Story.* Nazareth, Texas, January, 1975. (Limited to 400 Copies). [1] 2-19 [20]. Head of text, "The Estelline Story." Cover title ( ).

(51) *E. V. Sumner: Major-General United States Army: (1797-1863).* [Borger, Texas: Jim Hess Printers, 1969]. [i-v] i-vi [vii-ix] 1-382. Illus: print, "General E. V. Sumner From a painting by the author," [iii]. "Foreword," i-vi, datelined "Pep, Texas, October 18, 1968." "Bibliography," 345-363. "Index,"

364-382. Title on preliminary page [viii], "Gen. E. V. Sumner;" on spine, "E. V. Sumner: Major-General U. S. Army." Cloth, navy lettered in gold. Dust jacket: white background with reproduction of F. Stanley's portrait of General Sumner on front panel.

(52) *The Fairview, New Mexico Story (Present Winston, New Mexico)*. Pantex, Texas, June, 1962. Limited to 500 Copies. 1 [2] 3-20. "Forthcoming booklets on New Mexico Towns," 20. Head of text, "The Fairview, New Mexico Story." Cover title, "The Fairview (New Mexico) Story."

(53) *The Farley New Mexico Story*. Nazareth, Texas, March, 1972. (Limited to 400 Copies). 1 [2] 2-24. Head of text, "The Farley Story." Cover title ( ).

(54) *The Floyd, New Mexico Story*. Pep, Texas, February, 1967. (Limited to 400 Copies). 1 2-20. Head of text, "The Floyd, New Mexico, Story." Cover title ( ).

(55) *The Folsom, New Mexico Story*. Pantex, Texas, February, 1962. 1 [2] 3-20. Cover title ( ).

(56) *Fort Bascom: Comanche-Kiowa Barrier*. [Pampa, Texas: Pampa Print Shop, 1961]. [i-iv] i-v [vi] 1-224. "Dedicated to Col. Edward Bergman of Fort Bascom, N.M. Who Deserves a Niche in New Mexico's Hall of Fame," [ii]. "Foreword," i-iv, datelined "White Deer, Texas, May 3, 1960." "Notes and Comments," 10-19, 44-53, 80-96, 129-136, 160-170, 213-214. "Bibliography," 215-224. Cloth, yellow lettered in red. Dust jacket.

(57) *The Fort Conrad, New Mexico Story*. Dumas, Texas, May, 1961. 1 2-19 [20]. "Charles Magill Conrad" [biographical sketch], 2. Head of text, "Fort Conrad, New Mexico Story." Cover title ( ).

(58) *Fort Craig*. [Pampa, Texas: Pampa Print Shop, 1963]. [i-ii] i-ii [iii-iv] 1-204. "Foreword," i-ii, datelined "St. Francis—Pantex Community, October

2, 1962." "Ground Plan, Fort Craig, New Mexico by F. Stanley," 34-35. "Bibliography," 191-195. "Index," 197-204. Cloth, golden-yellow lettered in red. Dust jacket.

(59) *The Fort Fillmore, New Mexico Story.* Pantex, Texas, May, 1961. [LC: His New Mexico local history series]. 1 [2] 3-20. "Bibliography," 20. Head of text, "Fort Fillmore, New Mexico Story." Cover title ( ).

(60) *Fort Stanton.* [Pampa, Texas: Pampa Print Shop, 1964]. Limited to Five Hundred Copies. [i-viii] i-iv 1-263 [264]. "Foreword," i-iv, datelined "Pep, Texas —September 23, 1964." "Bibliography," 245-254. "Index," 255-263. Cover title, "Fort Stanton New Mexico." Cloth, yellow lettered in red. Dust jacket.

(61) *The Fort Thorn, New Mexico Story.* Pep, Texas, May, 1965. (Limited to 400 Copies). 1 [2] 3-20. Cover title ( ).

(62) *The Fort Tulerosa New Mexico Story.* Pep, Texas, August, 1968. (Limited to 400 Copies). 1 2-20. Head of text, "The Fort Tulerosa Story." Cover title ( ).

(63) *Fort Union (New Mexico).* [LC: Canadian, Texas, 1953]. [i-vi] vii-xiii [xiv] 1-305. Illus: 10 plates. "Dedicated to all those who are working to place the ruins of Fort Union in the Halls of Immortality . . .All other monuments were the work of outsiders looking in; this is the work of insiders looking out." "Foreword: Why Fort Union?" vii-xiii. "Bibliography," 301-305. Cloth, golden-yellow lettered in red. Dust jacket.

(64) *The French, New Mexico Story.* Pantex, Texas, October, 1962. Limited to 500 Copies. 1 [2] 3-20. Cover title ( ).

(65) *The Galisteo, New Mexico Story.* Pep, Texas, June, 1965. (Limited to 400 Copies). 1 [2] 3-20. Head of text, "The Galisteo, New Mexico, Story." Cover title ( ).

(66) *The Gardiner, New Mexico Story.* Pep, Texas, July,
1965. (Limited to 400 Copies). 1 [2] 3-26, b*l.* Illus:
10 prints. Cover title ( ).

(67) *The Georgetown, New Mexico Story.* Pep, Texas,
May, 1963. (Limited to 500 Copies). 1 [2] 3-20. Cover title ( ).

(68) *Giant in Lilliput: The Story of Donanciano Vigil.*
[Pampa, Texas: Pampa Print Shop, 1963]. [i-ii] i-
iv [v-vi] 1-219 [220]. "Foreword," i-iv. "Bibliography," 207-209. "Index," 211-219. Cloth, yellow with
red lettering. Dust jacket.

(69) *The Gladstone New Mexico Story.* Nazareth, Texas,
March, 1972. (Limited to 400 Copies). 1 [2] 3-22,
b*l.* Head of text, "The Gladstone Story." Cover
title ( ).

(70) *The Glenrio New Mexico Story.* Nazareth, Texas,
January, 1973. (Limited to 400 Copies). 1 [2] 3-23
[24]. Head of text, "The Glenrio Story." Cover
title ( ).

(71) *The Glorieta, New Mexico Story.* Pep, Texas, May,
1965. (Limited to 400 Copies). 1 [2] 3-22, b*l.* Cover title ( ).

(72) *The Golden, New Mexico Story.* Pep, Texas, June,
1964. (Limited to 400 Copies). 1 [2] 3-20. Cover
title ( ).

(73) *The Grady New Mexico Story.* Pep, Texas, August,
1968. (Limited to 400 Copies). 1 [2] 3-22, b*l.* Head
of text, "The Grady Story." Cover title ( ).

(74) *The Grafton New Mexico Story.* Nazareth, Texas,
January, 1973. (Limited to 400 Copies). 1 [2] 3-22,
b*l.* Head of text, "The Grafton Story." Cover
title ( ).

(75) *The Grant That Maxwell Bought.* [Denver: The
World Press, 1952. Limited Edition of The Grant
That Maxwell Bought; This Book Number. . .of an

edition limited to two hundred and fifty volumes].
[i-viii] 1-256, two columns per page. "Foreword,"
[vi], datelined "Pecos, New Mexico: February 22,
1952." Illus: "The Picture Story," 33 prints, 238-
252. "Bibliography," 254-256. Cloth, navy lettered
in gold.

(76) *The Grenville New Mexico Story.* Nazareth, Texas,
December, 1969. (Limited to 400 Copies). 1 [2] 3-
22, b*l.* Head of text, "The Grenville Story." Cover
title ( ).

(77) *The Grier, New Mexico Story.* Pep, Texas, June,
1965. (Limited to 400 Copies). 1 2-20. Head of text,
"The Grier, New Mexico, Story." Cover title ( ).

(78) *The Hermosa, New Mexico Story.* Pep, Texas, March,
1965. (Limited to 400 Copies). 1 [2], 3-20. Cover
title ( ).

(79) *The Higgins Texas Story.* Nazareth, Texas, January,
1975. (Limited to 400 Copies). [1] 2-20. Head of
text, "The Higgins Story." Cover title ( ).

(80) *The Hillsboro, New Mexico Story.* Pep, Texas, August, 1964. (Limited to 400 Copies). 1 2-20. Cover
title ( ).

(81) *Ike Stockton.* [Denver: World Press Inc., 1959].
"Limited Edition of which this is Copy No. . . . Signed
. . ." [i-viii] ix-x 1-169. "Dedicated to Dr. Frank
D. Reeve Who Said: History is the never ending
search for the closest approximation to the truth of
what happened, why it happened, and when it happened. It is governed by accepted canons of scholar-
ship. . .embellishing with a fine literary style enhances the pleasure of the reader, but the substance, not the style, is the prime consideration. . .
New Mexico Historical Review, April, 1965," [v].
"Foreword," ix-x, datelined "October, 1958, Rotan,
Texas." Cover title, "The Private War of Ike Stock-

ton." Cloth, golden-yellow lettered in red. Dust jacket.

(82) *The Inez, New Mexico Story.* Pep, Texas, April, 1967. (Limited to 400 Copies). 1 2-20. Head of text, "The Inez, New Mexico, Story." Cover title ( ).

(83) *The Isom, Texas Story.* Nazareth, Texas, November, 1973. (Limited to 400 Copies). 1 [2] 3-23 [24]. Head of text, "The Isom Story."

(84) *The Jicarilla Apaches of New Mexico: 1540-1967.* [Pampa, Texas: Pampa Print Shop, 1967]. —Limited to 500 Copies—. [i-iii] i-v [vi-vii] 1-376. "Foreword: The Jicarilla Apaches Then and Now," i-v. "Bibliography: Jicarillas of New Mexico," 355-365. "Index," 367-376. Title on spine, "The Jicarilla Apaches." Cloth, yellow lettered in red. Dust jacket.

(85) *Jim Courtright: Two Gun Marshal of Fort Worth* . . .in Collaboration with Lulu Courtright Hart, Henry Meyerhoff [and] Mrs. Henry Meyerhoff. [Denver: World Press, Inc., 1957]. [i-viii] ix-xii 1-234, b*l.* "Dedication To Henry and Maude, whose faith in a man the whole world sought to stigmatize as a gambler and racketeer weathered the test of time. He will gradually take his place among the great lawmen of the West," [v]. "Foreword," ix-xii, datelined "July 9, 1956, Rotan, Texas." Illus: "The Picture Story," 22 prints on eight unnumbered leaves between [228] and 229. "Bibliography," 229-234. Cover title, "Longhair Jim Courtright." There was a second printing of this title. Cloth, black lettered in silver. Dust jacket: photograph of Courtright on front panel.

(86) *The Johnson Mesa, New Mexico Story.* Pep, Texas, May, 1965. (Limited to 400 Copies). 1 [2] 3-22, b*l.* Head of text, "The Johnson Mesa, New Mexico, Story." Cover title ( ).

(87) *The Kelly New Mexico Story.* Nazareth, Texas, Jan-

uary, 1973. (Limited to 400 Copies). 1 2-24. Head of text, "The Kelly Story." Cover title ( ).

(88) *The Kenna, New Mexico Story.* Pep, Texas, March, 1966. (Limited to 400 Copies). 1 [2] 3-23 [24]. Head of text, "The Kenna, New Mexico, Story." Cover title ( ).

(89) *The Kingston, New Mexico Story.* Pantex, Texas, August, 1961. 1 [2] 3-20. Cover title ( ).

(90) *The Koehler, New Mexico Story.* Pep, Texas, August, 1964. (Limited to 400 Copies). 1 2-20. Cover title ( ).

(91) *The La Belle, New Mexico Story.* Pantex, Texas, October, 1962. Limited to 500 Copies. 1 [2] 3-19 [20]. Cover title ( ).

(92) *The Lake Valley, New Mexico Story.* Pep, Texas, March, 1964. (Limited to 400 Copies). 1 [2] 3-20. Cover title ( ).

(93) *The La Lande New Mexico Story.* Pep, Texas, March, 1969. (Limited to 400 Copies). 1 [2] 3-21 [22], b*l*. Head of text, "The La Lande Story." Cover title ( ).

(94) *The Lamy, New Mexico Story.* Pep, Texas, June, 1966. (Limited to 400 Copies). 1 2-20 Cover title ( ).

(95) *The Las Vegas Story (New Mexico).* [Denver: World Press, Inc., 1951]. [i-vi] vii [viii] ix-xi [xii] 1-340. Illus: 14 plates. "Dedicated to the Las Vegas Optic That Had The Courage To Survive," [v]. "Foreword," ix-xi, datelined "January 31, 1951, Pecos, N.M." "Bibliography," 335-340. Cover title, "The Las Vegas New Mexico Story." Cloth, green lettered in orange. Dust jacket.

(96) *The Lefors Texas Story.* Nazareth, Texas, January, 1975. (Limited to 400 Copies). [1] 2-20. Head of text, "The Lefors Story."

(97) *The Liberty New Mexico Story.* Nazareth, Texas, March, 1972. (Limited to 400 Copies). 1 [2] 3-24. Head of text, "The Liberty Story." Cover title ( ).

(98) *The Lincoln, New Mexico Story.* Pep, Texas, November, 1964. (Limited to 400 Copies). 1 [2] 3-26, b*l.* Cover title ( ).

(99) *The Lipscomb Texas Story.* Nazareth, Texas, January, 1975. (Limited to 400 Copies). [1] 2-20. Head of text, "The Lipscomb Story."

(100) *The Loma Parda New Mexico Story.* Nazareth, Texas, December, 1969. (Limited to 400 Copies). 1 [2] 3-22, b*l.* Head of text, "The Loma Parda Story." Cover title ( ).

(101) *The Los Alamos, New Mexico Story.* Pantex, Texas, November, 1961. 1 [2] 3-20. "Sources," 20. Cover title ( ).

(102) *The Magdalena New Mexico Story.* Nazareth, Texas, January, 1973. (Limited to 400 Copies). 1 [2] 3-23 [24]. Head of text, "The Magdalena Story." Cover title ( ).

(103) *The Manzano, New Mexico Story.* Pantex, Texas, June, 1962. Limited to 500 Copies. 1 [2] 3-19 [20]. Cover title ( ).

(104) *The Maxwell, New Mexico Story.* Pep, Texas, March, 1963. Limited to 500 Copies. 1 [2] 3-20. Cover title ( ).

(105) *The Melrose, New Mexico Story.* Pep, Texas, June, 1965. (Limited to 400 Copies). 1 2-20. Cover title ( ).

(106) *Mescalero Epic.* Nazareth, Texas, December, 1969. (Limited to 400 Copies). 1 2-20.

(107) *The Miami, New Mexico Story.* Pep, Texas, September, 1964. (Limited to 400 Copies). 1 2-20. Cover title ( ).

(108) *The Miami Texas Story.* Nazareth, Texas, August, 1974. (Limited to 400 Copies). 1 2-22, b*l.* Head of text, "The Miami Story."

(109) *The Milnesand New Mexico Story.* Pep, Texas, August, 1968. (Limited to 400 Copies). 1 [2] 3-23 [24]. Head of text, "The Milnesand Story." Cover title ( ).

(110) *The Mogollon New Mexico Story.* Pep, Texas, August, 1968. (Limited to 400 Copies). 1 [2] 3-23 [24]. Head of text, "The Mogollon Story." Cover title ( ).

(111) *The Montezuma, New Mexico Story.* Pep, Texas, August, 1963. (Limited to 500 Copies). 1 [2] 3-20. Cover title ( ).

(112) *The Mora, New Mexico Story.* Pep, Texas, August, 1963. (Limited to 500 Copies). 1 2-20. Cover title ( ).

(113) *The Mosquero New Mexico Story.* Nazareth, Texas, December, 1970. (Limited to 400 Copies). 1 2-24. Head of text, "The Mosquero Story." Cover title ( ).

(114) *The Nambe, New Mexico Story.* Pep, Texas, April, 1966. (Limited to 400 Copies). 1 2-20. Cover title ( ).

(115) *The Nara Visa New Mexico Story.* Nazareth, Texas, March, 1972. (Limited to 400 Copies). 1 [2] 3-24. Head of text, "The Nara Visa Story." Cover title ( ).

(116) *No Tears for Black Jack Ketchum.* [Denver: World Press, Inc., 1958]. "Only 500 Copies Printed Of which this is Copy No. . . ." [i-viii] ix-x 1-148. "Dedicated to the Staff of the Museum Library at Santa Fe, N.M. For their cooperation, help and time," [v]. "Foreword," ix-x, datelined "Rotan, Texas, October 9, 1957." "Bibliography," 147-148. Paper, black lettered in silver.

(117) *Notes On Joel Fowler.* Pep, Texas, March, 1963. Limited to 500 Copies. 1 2-19 [20]. "Foreword," 2.

(118) *The Odyssey of Juan Archibeque.* Pantex, Texas, November, 1962. Limited to 500 Copies. 1 2-20. "Foreword," 2. "Postscript," 20.

(119) *One Half Mile from Heaven or The Cimarron Story.*
Compiled. . .for The Raton Historical Society. [Denver: World Press, 1949]. [i-xii] 3-155 [156], bl.
Illus: 9 plates. "Dedicated to the people of Cimarron who love their history," [v]. "Acknowledgements. . .Special recognition is given Joe Apache for the cover design. . . ," [vii]. "Bibliography," 145-147. "Footnotes," 148-155. Cover: gray paper with cover drawing by Joe Apache of a ram in a mountain scene.

(120) *The Otero, New Mexico Story.* Pantex, Texas, April, 1962. Limited to 500 Copies. 1 [2] 3-20. Cover title ( ).

(121) *The Perryton Texas Story.* Nazareth, Texas, January, 1975. (Limited to 400 Copies). [1] 2-19 [20]. Head of text, "The Perryton Story."

(122) *The Phillips Texas Story.* Nazareth, Texas, January, 1975. (Limited to 400 Copies). [1] 2-20. Head of text, "The Phillips Story."

(123) *The Picuris, New Mexico Story.* Pantex, Texas, October, 1962. Limited to 500 Copies. 1 2-20.

(124) *The Plemons (Texas) Story.* Nazareth, Texas, November, 1973. (Limited to 400 Copies). 1 [2] 3-22, bl. Head of text, "The Plemons Story."

(125) *The Pojoaque, New Mexico Story.* Pep, Texas, June, 1965. (Limited to 400 Copies). 1 2-20. Cover title ( ).

(126) *El Potrero de Chimayo New Mexico.* Nazareth, Texas, December, 1969. (Limited to 400 Copies). 1 [2] 3-22, bl. Head of text, "Potrero de Chimayo." Cover title, "El Potrero de Chimayo, New Mexico."

(127) *The Puerto de Luna New Mexico Story.* Nazareth, Texas, December, 1969. (Limited to 400 Copies). 1 [2] 3-22, bl. Head of text, "The Puerto de Luna Story." Cover title ( ).

(128) *The Questa, New Mexico Story.* Pantex, Texas, Oct-

ober, 1962. Limited to 500 Copies. 1 [2] 3-20. Cover title ( ).

(129) *Raton Chronicle.* Compiled. . .for Raton Historical Society. [Denver: World Press Publishing Co., 1948]. [i-xvi] 3-146. Illus: 9 prints. "Imprimatur + Edwin V. Byrne, D. D. Archbishop of Santa Fe, Santa Fe, April 21, 1948, Nihil Obstat Angelico Chavez, O.F.M. Censor Deputatus," [iii]. "Dedicated to The Boys who lost their lives in World War II. Wherever they lie, There is a little Bit of Raton," [vii]. "Acknowledgements," [xi]. "Footnotes," 133-143. "Bibliography," 144-146. Tipped-in leaf with holograph note, "Thanks a million for the order—Enclosed. . .copies as ordered, F. Stanley." Paper, beige with red lettering and drawing of large rat examining bound newspaper volume opened to "Raton Chronicle."

(130) *The Red River, New Mexico Story.* Pantex, Texas, November, 1962. Limited to 500 Copies. 1 [2] 3-20. Cover title ( ).

(131) *The Reserve (New Mexico) Story.* Nazareth, Texas, November, 1973. (Limited to 400 Copies). 1 [2] 3-20. Head of text, "The Reserve Story." Cover title ( ).

(132) *Rodeo Town (Canadian, Texas).* [Denver: The World Press, Inc., 1953]. [i-vi] vii [viii] ix-xii 1-418, b*l.* "Dedicated to T. A. Vigil whose untiring efforts in research and note taking made this book possible," [vi]. "Foreword," ix-xii, datelined "Canadian, Texas, April 10, 1953." Illus: "Picture Story," 29 prints on 8 unnumbered leaves between 260 and 261. Title on preliminary page [v], "Rodeo Town;" on cover, "Rodeo Town Canadian, Texas." Cloth, navy with silver lettering. Dust jacket.

(133) *The Rogers, New Mexico Story.* Pep, Texas, April, 1967. (Limited to 400 Copies). 1 [2] 3-23 [24]. Cover title ( ).

(134) *The Roy New Mexico Story*. Nazareth, Texas, March, 1972. (Limited to 400 Copies). 1 [2] 3-24. Head of text, "The Roy Story." Cover title ( ).

(135) *The San Antonio (New Mexico) Story*. Nazareth, Texas, November, 1973. (Limited to 400 Copies). 1 2-20. Head of text, "The San Antonio Story."

(136) *The Sandia New Mexico Story*. Pep, Texas, August, 1968. (Limited to 400 Copies). 1 [2] 3-23 [24]. Head of text, "The Sandia Story." Cover title ( ).

(137) *The San Ildefonso New Mexico Story*. Nazareth, Texas, December, 1969. (Limited to 400 Copies). 1 2-23 [24]. Head of text, "The San Ildefonso Story." Cover title ( ).

(138) *The San Juan New Mexico Story*. Nazareth, Texas, December, 1970. (Limited to 400 Copies). 1 [2] 3-23 [24]. Head of text, "The San Juan Story." Cover title ( ).

(139) *The San Marcial (New Mexico) Story*. [I.C: White Deer, Texas, May 31, 1960]. [i-ii] 1-18. "Foreword," [i], datelined "White Deer, Texas, May 31, 1960." Head of text, "The San Marcial, N. Mexico Story."

(140) *The San Miguel del Bado New Mexico Story*. Pep, Texas, September, 1964. (Limited to 400 Copies). 1 2-20. Head of text, "San Miguel del Bado, New Mexico Story." Cover title ( ).

(141) *The Sapello New Mexico Story*. Nazareth, Texas, December, 1970. (Limited to 400 Copies). 1 [2] 3-23 [24]. Head of text, "The Sapello Story." Cover title ( ).

(142) *Satanta and the Kiowas*. [Borger, Texas: Jim Hess Printers, 1968]. [i-v] i-iv [v-vii] [1]-391 [392]. Illus: print of photograph, "Set-tainte or Satanta (White Bear)," [iii]; caption on facing page, " 'A Kiowa placed in a Pen Dies' (Words spoken by Chief

Satanta during the Medicine Lodge peace talks)," [ii]. "Foreword," i-iv, datelined "Pep, Texas, November, 1967." "Bibliography," 363-377. "Index," 378-391. Leaf numbered 21/22 bound upside down between pages 26 and 29; leaf numbered 27/28 upside down between 20 and 23. Cloth, yellow lettered in black. Dust jacket.

(143) *The Seven Rivers, New Mexico Story.* Pep, Texas, January, 1963. (Limited to 500 Copies). 1 2-20. Cover title ( ).

(144) *The Signal Hill (Texas) Story.* Nazareth, Texas, November, 1973. 1 [2] 3-22, b*l.* Head of text, "The Signal Hill Story."

(145) *The Silverton Texas Story.* Nazareth, Texas, January, 1975. (Limited to 400 Copies). [1] 2-20. Head of text, "The Silverton Story."

(146) *The Shakespeare, New Mexico Story.* Pantex, Texas, October, 1961. 1 [2] 3-20. Cover title ( ).

(147) *The Skellytown Texas Story.* Nazareth, Texas, August, 1974. (Limited to 400 Copies). 1 2-22, b*l.* Head of text, "The Skellytown Story."

(148) *Socorro: The Oasis.* [Denver: World Press, Inc., 1950]. [i-xviii] 1-221 [222]. Illus: 10 plates. "A Raton Historical Society Publication," [vii]. "Dedicated to Friar Alonzo Benavides, Who named the town Socorro in honor of Nuestra Senora [*sic*] del Socorro, and Juan Onate [*sic*], who used the name in another locality before him," [ix]. "Foreword," [xi-xiv], datelined "March 1, 1950." "Bibliography," 215-221. Title on preliminary page [iii], "Socorro —The Oasis;" on cover, "Socorro the Oasis." Cloth, golden-yellow lettered in red. Small number bound in light blue cloth lettered in darker blue. Dust jacket: yellow lettered in black, displaying photograph of church tower.

(149) *The Sofia New Mexico Story.* Nazareth, Texas, De-

cember, 1970. (Limited to 400 Copies). Head of text, "The Sofia Story." Cover title ( ).

(150) *The Springer, New Mexico Story.* Pantex, Texas, January, 1962. 1 2-24. Cover title ( ).

(151) *The Stinnett Texas Story.* Nazareth, Texas, August, 1974. (Limited to 400 Copies). 1 2-21 [22], b*l.* Head of text, "The Stinnett Story."

(152) *Story of the Texas Panhandle Railroads.* [Borger, Texas: Hess Publishing Co., 1976]. [i-iv] i-xii [xiii-xvi] 1-456. "Foreword," i-[xiii], datelined "Atwater, California, June 23, 1974." "Bibliography," 423-438. "Index," 439-456. Cloth, light blue lettered in black. Dust jacket: cream background lettered in brown with title, "Railroads of the Texas Panhandle."

(153) *The St. Vrain, New Mexico Story.* Pep, Texas, June, 1966. (Limited to 400 Copies). 1 2-20. Cover title ( ).

(154) *The Sugarite, New Mexico Story.* Pep, Texas, June, 1964. (Limited to 400 Copies). 1 2-20. Cover title ( ).

(155) *The Taiban New Mexico Story.* Pep, Texas, January, 1969. (Limited to 400 Copies). 1 2-20. Head of text, "The Taiban Story." Cover title ( ).

(156) *The Tatum New Mexico Story.* Pep, Texas, November, 1968. (Limited to 500 Copies). 1 2-24. Head of text, "The Tatum Story." Cover title ( ).

(157) *The Tesuque, New Mexico Story.* Pep, Texas, September, 1963. (Limited to 400 Copies). 1 2-20. Cover title ( ).

(158) *The Texas Panhandle From Cattlemen to Feed Lots.* [Borger, Texas: Jim Hess Printers, 1971]. —Limited to 500 Copies—. [i-xii] i-xx [xxi-xxii] 1-656. "Foreword," [vii-x], datelined "Nazareth, Texas." "Introduction," i-xx. "Appendix I: Post Offices in Certain Counties in Texas," 595-599. "Appendix II: From

Lubbock Avalanche-Journal, March 4, 1971," 600-602. "Bibliography," 603-623. "Index," 625-656. Cloth, light blue lettered in black. Dust jacket: cream background lettered in brown with title "The Texas Panhandle From Cattlemen to Feed Lots (1880-1970)."

(159) *The Texico, New Mexico Story*. Pep, Texas, April, 1966. (Limited to 400 Copies). 1 2-20. Head of text, "The Texico, New Mexico, Story." Cover title ( ).

(160) *The Texline Texas Story*. Nazareth, Texas, January, 1975. (Limited to 400 Copies). [1] 2-19 [20]. Head of text, "The Texline Story."

(161) *The Tex Thornton Story*. Nazareth, Texas, January, 1975. (Limited to 400 Copies). [1] 2-19 [20].

(162) *The Thomas Oliver Boggs Story*. Nazareth, Texas. March, 1972. (Limited to 400 Copies). 1 [2] 3-23 [24].

(163) *The Tiptonville New Mexico Story*. Nazareth, Texas, January, 1973. (Limited to 400 Copies). 1 [2] 3-23 [24]. Head of text, "The Tiptonville Story." Cover title ( ).

(164) *The Tolar, New Mexico Story*. Pep, Texas, April, 1967. (Limited to 400 Copies). 1 2-20. Head of text, "The Tolar, New Mexico, Story. Cover title ( ).

(165) *The Tome, New Mexico Story*. Pep, Texas, June. 1966. (Limited to 400 Copies). 1 [2] 3-22, b*l*. Cover title ( ).

(166) *The Umbarger Texas Story*. Nazareth, Texas, August, 1974. (Limited to 400 Copies). 1 2-21 [22], b*l*. Head of text, "The Umbarger Story."

(167) *The Van Houten, New Mexico Story*. Pep, Texas, October, 1964. (Limited to 400 Copies). 1 [2] 3-22, b*l*. Cover title ( ).

(168) *The Vega Texas Story*. Nazareth, Texas, January,

1975. (Limited to 400 Copies). [1] 2-20. Head of text, "The Vega Story."

(169) *The Villanueva New Mexico Story*. Nazareth, Texas, December, 1970. (Limited to 400 Copies). 1 2-24. Head of text, "The Villanueva Story." Cover title ( ).

(170) *The Wagon Mound New Mexico Story*. Pep, Texas, August, 1968. (Limited to 400 Copies). 1 [2] 3-24. Head of text, "The Wagon Mound Story." Cover title ( ).

(171) *The Wallace, New Mexico Story*. Pantex, Texas, October, 1962. Limited to 500 Copies. 1 [2] 3-20. Head of text, "The Wallace, New Mexico Story (Present Domingo)." Cover title ( ).

(172) *The Watrous, New Mexico Story*. Pantex, Texas, August, 1962. Limited to 500 Copies. 1 [2] 3-20. Cover title ( ).

(173) *The White Deer Texas Story*. Nazareth, Texas, August, 1974. (Limited to 400 Copies). 1 2-21 [22], b*l*. Head of text, "The White Deer Story."

(174) *The White Oaks (New Mexico) Story*. [LC: White Deer, Texas, 1963]. 1 2-23 [24]. Head of text, "The White Oaks, New Mexico, Story."

(175) *The Yankee, New Mexico Story*. Pep, Texas, July, 1964. (Limited to 400 Copies). 1 2-20. Cover title ( ).

(176) *The Yeso New Mexico Story*. Pep, Texas, January, 1969. (Limited to 400 Copies). 1 [2] 3-20. Head of text, "The Yeso Story." Cover title ( ).

(177) *The Zia New Mexico Story*. Pep, Texas, January, 1969. (Limited to 400 Copies). 1 [2] 3-22, b*l*. Head of text, "The Zia Story." Cover title ( ).

In the following notes, citations to titles by F. Stanley do not include a reference to the author, as this is assumed to be understood, nor to date and place of publication, which may be found in the bibliography. Much information has been based on oral history interviews with Father Stanley, but every effort has been made to verify statements of fact in other sources.

1. *Jim Courtright: Two Gun Marshal of Fort Worth,* p. x.

2. Personal interview with Stanley Francis Louis Crocchiola, recorded by Edward Richter, Judy Hiner and Joseph Place in Pep, Texas, ca. 1969, typed transcript, p. 20 (hereafter cited as First Interview). Personal interview with Stanley Francis Louis Crocchiola, recorded by the author and Pearce S. Grove in Portales, New Mexico, July 14, 1975, typed transcript, pp. 2-3 (hereafter cited as Second Interview). Both interviews available in Golden Library, Eastern New Mexico University, Portales, New Mexico. Alaska and Canada had a series of gold rushes in the period spanning 1880-98, so Vincent Crocchiola could have saved his money and embarked as early as 1888 ("Juneau, Alaska," *Encyclopedia Americana,* 1983 ed.).

3. First Interview, p. 20; Second Interview, p. 3; Crocchiola to Walker, September 28, 1983 (available in Golden Library). Renee Paul Chambellan is credited with all metal sculpture in the Rockefeller Center complex, including that in Radio City Music Hall (*Who Was Who in America,* III, p. 147).

4. Second Interview, pp. 3-5; back of dust jacket, *Socorro: The Oasis.* Father Stanley may be 5' 3" tall.

5. Second Interview, pp. 5-6. Stanley Crocchiola to Most Reverend R. A. Gerken, October 31, 1940; S. Mary Loyola Maestas, Archivist, Archdiocese of Santa Fe, to Walker, January 5, 1984 (copies of both letters available

in Golden Library). The Motherhouse of the Friars of the Atonement is St. Paul's Friary, Graymoor, located in Garrison, N.Y. In the letter to Gerken, F. Stanley said that he attended, and taught at, Graymoor, rather than St. John's, the name that he consistently used for the academy in both interviews. Evidently it no longer exists under either name, however (*Catholic Almanac,* 1981 ed., p. 531).

6. Second Interview, pp. 5-6.

7. First Interview, p. 1; Second Interview, p. 2; Crocchiola to Gerken, October 31, 1940.

8. Crocchiola to Billy M. Jones, quoted in Jones, *Health-Seekers in the Southwest* (Norman: University of Oklahoma Press, 1967), p. 204; *The Texas Panhandle From Cattlemen to Feed Lots,* p. [1]. Father Stanley's account of his movements, from the time of his ordination until he settled in New Mexico, differs slightly among the various sources cited here as well as those in note 5.

9. First Interview, p. 20; Second Interview, pp. 6-7, 10-11. R. E. Lucey served as bishop of the Amarillo diocese from 1934-41 (*Who's Who in Texas,* 1947 ed., pp. 799-800).

10. First Interview, p. 2; Second Interview, pp. 7, 11.

11. *Ciudad Santa Fe,* III, p. viii; Maestas to Walker, January 5, 1984.

12. Maestas to Walker, January 5, 1984; Second Interview, p. 13. Byrne succeeded Gerken as archbishop of Santa Fe in 1943 (*Who's Who in Texas,* 1947 ed., p. 1077).

13. First Interview, pp. 8-10. Father Stanley did not say which schools approached him.

14. Second Interview, pp. 8-9, 12; Dust jacket, *Socorro: The Oasis.*

15. For a general discussion of regionalism in New Mexico, see Arrel M. Gibson, *The Santa Fe and Taos Colonies: Age of the Muses, 1900-1942* (Norman: University of Oklahoma Press, 1983).

16. *The Jicarilla Apaches of New Mexico,* p. ix.

17. First Interview, pp. 2, 3, 7; Second Interview, p. 9. Paul Horgan estimates the time of Lamy's arrival in Santa Fe as June 1851 (*Lamy of Santa Fe: His Life and Times* [New York: Farrar, Straus, 1975], p. 421).

18. First Interview, p. 2; Second Interview, p. 10.

19. *The Yeso, New Mexico Story,* p. 5.

20. First Interview, pp. 18, 20; Second Interview, p.12; *The Las Vegas Story (New Mexico),* p. x; *Dave Rudabaugh: Border Ruffian,* p. vi.

21. Second Interview, p. 14. Interestingly, though, *Raton Chronicle* did apparently have the Archbishop's approv-

al; see "Imprimatur" quoted in entry for *Raton Chronicle* in bibliography.

22. Second Interview, pp. 14, 21; First Interview, p. 4.

23. First Interview, p. 8; Second Interview, p. 10.

24. *Fort Bascom,* pp. iv-v; Second Interview, pp. 10, 14.

25. Maestas to Walker, January 19, 1984; First Interview, p. 2; Second Interview, pp. 7-8. FitzSimon succeeded Lucey as bishop of Amarillo in October 1941 (*Who's Who in Texas,* 1947 ed., p. 606).

26. Second Interview, pp. 7-8, 16.

27. *Ibid.,* pp. 8-10. Records in the archdiocese of Santa Fe show that Father Stanley resigned officially from that jurisdiction on April 1, 1952, and was incardinated into the diocese of Amarillo on April 14, 1952 (Maestas to Walker, January 5, 1984).

28. Second Interview, pp. 15-16; *The Phoenix (Formerly Montezuma),* descriptive brochure, reprinted (Las Vegas, New Mexico: La Galeria de los Artesanos, 1982), pp. [i-xii]. The Jesuit fathers went back to Mexico in 1972; in 1981 Armand Hammer bought the site for United World College of the American West, which opened for classes in the Fall of 1982 (promotional literature from the college).

29. Second Interview, p. 16. Unfortunately F. Stanley prepared his manuscript before photocopiers became standard office equipment.

30. Second Interview, p. 15; *The Texas Panhandle From Cattlemen to Feed Lots,* p. [ii]. Volume Seven by Castañeda, subtitled *The Church in Texas Since Independence,* makes no direct mention of F. Stanley's contributions, but in the preface Castañeda thanks "the Chanceries of the different dioceses. . .for their valuable cooperation," p. [x].

31. First Interview, p. 11; Second Interview, pp. 8, 16-17. FitzSimon died in July 1958 (*Who Was Who in America,* III, p. 258).

32. Second Interview, p. 12; Crocchiola to Walker, July 23, 1983; Rev. Msgr. Richard F. Vaughn, Chancellor, Diocese of Amarillo, to Walker, February 17, 1984 (both letters available in Golden Library).

33. First Interview, p. 9; Second Interview, pp. 12-13, 16.

34. Dust jacket, *Socorro: The Oasis; E. V. Sumner: Major-General United States Army,* p. [iii]. The 1971 book on Texas was the first of his surveys, *The Texas Panhandle From Cattlemen to Feed Lots.*

35. First Interview, p. 4; Second Interview, pp. 18, 20.

36. First Interview, p. 5; Second Interview, pp. 20-21.

37. Second Interview, p. 22; *The Texas Panhandle From Cattlemen to Feed Lots*, p. [ii]; *Story of the Texas Panhandle Railroads*, p. 1.

38. *The Texas Panhandle From Cattlemen to Feed Lots*, p. xx; Second Interview, p. 22; Crocchiola to Walker, July 23, 1983.

39. *The San Marcial (New Mexico) Story*, p. [i]. This work was therefore the first of the booklets to display his New Mexico colors, while of course these colors appeared earlier on the first of his clothbound books to carry them, *Socorro: The Oasis*.

40. *Book Talk*, X (August 1981), p. 3. See also lists of forthcoming works on back pages of some booklets (for instance *The Fairview, New Mexico Story*, p. 20), and in preliminary pages and on dust jackets of longer works.

41. *Ike Stockton*, p. 1; *The Golden, New Mexico Story*, p. 1; *The Miami Texas Story*, p. 1; *The Fort Tulerosa New Mexico Story*, p. 20.

42. *The Inez, New Mexico Story*, p. 2; *The Fairview, New Mexico Story*, p. 3; *The Manzano, New Mexico Story*, p. 19; *The Hermosa, New Mexico Story*, p. 3; *No Tears for Black Jack Ketchum*, p. [vi]; and the back of the dust jacket on *Jim Courtright*, mentioned the projected "Encyclopedia of New Mexico."

43. *The Chilili, New Mexico Story*, p. 20; *The Brilliant, New Mexico Story*, p. 26; *The Capulin New Mexico Story*, p. 24; *The Grenville, New Mexico Story*, p. 22.

44. *The Glenrio New Mexico Story*, p. 23; *The Elida, New Mexico Story*, p. 22; *The Hillsboro, New Mexico Story*, p. 20; *The Gardiner, New Mexico Story*, p. 26.

45. *Jim Courtright: Two Gun Marshal of Fort Worth*, p. xi; *Rodeo Town (Canadian Texas)*, p. x; *Dave Rudabaugh: Border Ruffian*, p. vii. Of interest here too is F. Stanley's quotation from Frank D. Reeves, "embellishing with a fine literary style enhances the pleasure of the reader, but the substance, not the style, is the prime consideration [of history]," *Ike Stockton*, p. [v].

46. *The Glenrio New Mexico Story*, p. 23; First Interview, pp. 12, 14-15, 17.

47. First Interview, p. 7; *Notes on Joel Fowler*, p. 2; *Desperadoes of New Mexico*, p. xi.

48. First Interview, pp. 3, 6-7, 18. Ever since territorial days (1889), New Mexico has had a law requiring county clerks to subscribe to and preserve one copy of each issue of every newspaper published within county lines, but

they have not always done so (*New Mexico Statutes Annotated,* 4-40-7, 4-40-8).

49. *The Las Vegas Story (New Mexico),* p. x; First Interview, p. 4. Father Stanley probably meant *The Jicarilla Apaches of New Mexico.*

50. First Interview, pp. 2, 7, 18; *Giant in Lilliput,* p. iv; *The Las Vegas Story (New Mexico),* p. ix.

51. First Interview, p. 8; Second Interview, pp. 21-23; *Dave Rudabaugh: Border Ruffian,* p. vii.

52. Second Interview, p. 18. Father Stanley had evidently forgotten Doughty's first name.

53. Second Interview, p. 18.

54. *Ibid,* p. 19.

55. *Giant in Lilliput,* p. v; *Fort Bascom,* p. iv.

56. Second Interview, p. 20.

57. First Interview, p. 5.

58. *Ibid.,* pp. 4-5. Recently (1982) an out-of-print catalog listed a copy of *Raton Chronicle* for $300.

59. *Ibid.,* pp. 7-8.

60. Second Interview, p. 21; *Rodeo Town (Canadian Texas),* p. [vi]. In the dedication of *Ciudad Santa Fe,* Volume I, F. Stanley also refers to "T. A. Vigil who helped translate ancient documents," p. [v].

61. J. Frank Dobie, *Guide to Life and Literature of the Southwest* (Dallas: Southern Methodist University Press, 1952), p. 109; Walter S. Campbell, *The Book Lover's Southwest: A Guide to Good Reading* (Norman: University of Oklahoma Press, 1955), p. 69; Jack D. Rittenhouse, *The Santa Fe Trail: A Historical Bibliography* (Albuquerque: University of New Mexico Press, 1971), p. 197; Ramon Adams, *Burs Under the Saddle: A Second Look at Books and Histories of the West* (Norman: University of Oklahoma Press, 1964), pp. 476-486.

62. Second Interview, p. 22.

63. Adams, p. vii.

64. *Ibid.,* pp. 476, 478, 480, 484-485.

65. First Interview, pp. 3, 5, 6; *Desperadoes of New Mexico,* p. 167.

66. First Interview, p. 6.

67. *The Clayton (New Mexico) Story,* p. 42; *The Jicarilla Apaches of New Mexico,* pp. iii-iv.

68. *The Odyssey of Juan Archibeque,* p. 2. F. Stanley had access to copies of the Archives of the Indies in libraries of the Amarillo diocese and Montezuma Seminary *(Ciudad Santa Fe,* I, p. [v]).

69. *The Clovis, New Mexico, Story,* p. 256; First In-

terview, p. 6; *The Apaches of New Mexico*, p. iv.

70. *Jim Courtright*, p. xi.

71. *The San Marcial (New Mexico) Story*, p. 15; *The Gladstone New Mexico Story*, pp. 5-6, 8-9, 11, 13, 16-17, 20.

72. *The Clovis, New Mexico, Story*, pp. iv-v.

73. *The Milnesand New Mexico Story*, p. 3. Term is from "This is the Brigadoon section of New Mexico," *The Villanueva, New Mexico Story*, p. 2.

74. *The Grant That Maxwell Bought*, p. 1; *The Apaches of New Mexico*, p. 1; *Satanta and the Kiowas*, p. i; *The Plemons (Texas) Story*, p. 3; *The Otero, New Mexico Story*, p. 20; *The Catskill, New Mexico Story*, p. 20; *The Grafton New Mexico Story*, p. 22.

75. *Jim Courtright*, p. x; *Dave Rudabaugh*, pp. vi-vii.

76. *The Duke City: The Story of Albuquerque, New Mexico*, p. xii; *Satanta and the Kiowas*, p. iv.

77. Phrases from *Dave Rudabaugh: Border Ruffian*, p. viii; and "Ah, but a man's reach should exceed his grasp, / Or what's a heaven for?" from Robert Browning, "Andrea del Sarto."

78. Phrases from *The Glenrio New Mexico Story*, p. 23; and Adams, p. 482.

79. With their Zia symbols, and gold and red colors, Father Stanley's New Mexico booklets look like miniature state flags. "Those are the colors of the royal house of Spain," he said; "that's where the colors of the New Mexico flag came from." Father Stanley said that he selected the colors of his Texas booklets to represent "the blue flag of Texas with the lone star in the blue shield." The motif of three squares has no significance, however; "those were just embellishments by the printer who thought perhaps the cover was too bare." Second Interview, pp. 19-20.

80. *Book Talk*, X (August 1981), 1. Further mention of "Cuidad Santa Fe" appears in lists of forthcoming books, for instance on p. vi of *No Tears for Black Jack Ketchum* and back of dust jacket for *The Apaches of New Mexico*.

81. Laura V. Monti to Walker, July 14, 1983 (available in Golden Library).

While not an exact replica, this book keeps as faithfully as possible to the spirit of books by F. Stanley, which had a consistency of style which we have attempted to follow. The 5½" x 8½" page size and Century Expanded type are typical, as are the yellow cover and dust jacket printed (or stamped) in red. The title page and headings adhere to the F. Stanley style, as well. *The F. Stanley Story* was designed and typeset by Jene Lyon at The Lightning Tree in Santa Fe County, New Mexico, in 1984.

The signature on the front flyleaf is a facsimile of a typical F. Stanley autograph, this example taken from a copy of his 1963 book, *The Duke City*.